SECURITY MOM

An Unclassified Guide to Protecting
Our Homeland and Your Home

JULIETTE KAYYEM

SIMON & SCHUSTER

New York   London   Toronto   Sydney   New Delhi

Simon & Schuster
1230 Avenue of the Americas
New York, NY 10020

Copyright © 2016 by Juliette Kayyem

First Simon & Schuster hardcover edition April 2016

SIMON & SCHUSTER and colophon are
registered trademarks of Simon & Schuster, Inc.

For information about special discounts for bulk purchases,
please contact Simon & Schuster Special Sales
at 1-866-506-1949 or business@simonandschuster.com.

The Simon & Schuster Speakers Bureau can bring authors to your live event.
For more information or to book an event, contact the
Simon & Schuster Speakers Bureau at 1-866-248-3049 or
visit our website at www.simonspeakers.com.

Interior design by Ruth Lee-Mui

Manufactured in the United States of America

10 9 8 7 6 5 4 3 2 1

Library of Congress Cataloging-in-Publication Data is available.

ISBN 978-1-4767-3374-6
ISBN 978-1-4767-3377-7 (ebook)

To David,
my heart's home

To Cecilia, Leo, and Jeremiah,
my home's heartbeat

We oughtn't pray for what we've never known
And humanity has never known
Unbroken peace
Unmixed blessing
No.
Better to pray for . . .
The will to see and touch
The power to do good and make new.

—Rabbi Stanley F. Chyet,
as found in *Mishkan
T'filah: A Reform Siddur*

SECURITY MOM

PROLOGUE

I STARED AT THE TRAFFIC LIGHT. RED. THE RADIO WAS OFF—NONE OF THOSE TOP 40 tunes I blasted even when the kids had left the car. Instead, I listened to the low thrum of the motor, the echoes of sirens, the lub-dub of my heart. It was nearing midnight on Thursday, April 18, 2013, the rhythm of a surreal week in Boston moving closer to a weekend that promised no relief: multiple bombings on Monday; police, FBI agents, reporters, and news teams a mile from our house for days; a nation descended into grief and fear; a global investigation of two men who turned out to be our neighbors.

My kids—Cecilia, Leo, and Jeremiah—were home. Their April-break vacation had been canceled, because Mom's job was . . . what, exactly? I was no longer in government, no longer the state's—this Commonwealth of Massachusetts's—homeland security advisor, no

1

longer a senior appointee in the Obama administration at the Department of Homeland Security. I had no actual responsibility except, after answering a call from a friend at CNN ("Is this Juliette? Where are you? Can you get to Commonwealth Avenue?"), to explain to others what I knew, since those bombs went off at the very marathon I had worked so hard to secure years before.

As a homeland security and counterterrorism expert, I have learned to compartmentalize the despair that follows disaster. My role isn't to feel too much—though I so often do—but to plan, and prepare, and respond to whatever mayhem, as it always does, has arrived.

But this—this act of terror—hit close to home. My son, playing outside that day, heard the explosion. Later that night, helicopters hovering over our house kept us awake, as if we could even think of sleep. I still had a panicked voice message on my phone from a friend who crossed the finish line two minutes before the bombs went off, who then spent another endless twenty-three minutes searching for her husband and two children.

That Thursday, I spent all day on the air. At five p.m., the FBI released images of the men they suspected were the terrorists, but they had no more evidence and asked the public for help with identification. Who were they? Someone must know.

It turned out that the Tsarnaev brothers were not strangers to this city. They lived down the street from us. They had attended my kids' school. They visited a mosque that we passed every day. Had we seen them at the market once or twice? Those brothers fit so easily into our eclectic Cambridge neighborhood—as did we, as did so many others from around the globe seeking the acceptance of this progressive enclave in the shadows of Harvard and MIT.

But no one knew any of this that Thursday night. So I left the makeshift CNN bureau near the marathon finish line a few hours after the FBI made their request. I retrieved my car from the hotel where every newscaster had set up—and where groupies came to take photos of Anderson Cooper or Chris Cuomo—and drove home toward Cambridge. It was then, just a hundred feet from my highway exit, on an almost empty road, that I could feel—before I heard—the rush of police cars come up on me from behind: one, two, three, then maybe forty cop cars passing me and driving toward Watertown. Something was happening. I pulled over, not needing instruction, as I watched them—one after another after another—head somewhere down the road. Then total silence again, like an elephant stampede that leaves nothing in its wake. I waited by the side of the road, hoping for the "all clear"—the public safety lingo that had become part of my life—but none ever came.

I just waited, at a complete standstill on the highway. I could just as easily have been parked. My cell phone rang. It was David, my husband, calling.

I imagined David was pacing in the downstairs kitchen of our home. I couldn't help but wonder if the kids could sleep through all the noise. At ages eleven, nine, and seven, Cecilia, Leo, and Jeremiah were no longer climbing into our bed when they had bad dreams, but this had to affect them, I knew. It certainly affected every adult. David, worried, wanted to know when I was getting home. Now seemed like a pretty good time, I thought.

I started the car, inched slowly toward the exit and through the tollbooth, and waited for the light at the end of the ramp to turn green. My cell phone rang again. I saw the familiar 404 area code on my screen: an Atlanta number. "Can you come back?" my handler—every profession has its own code words—from CNN asked, explaining they were setting up to go live on air again. A massive search appeared to be underway, she said with a hint of excitement about what was about to unfold. I didn't feel any of her adrenaline rush; I had witnessed the beginning of the chase here on the highway, and was too tired from all that the brothers had unleashed in such proximity to my home. Producers wanted me in the makeshift studio in full expert mode, ready to discuss the lessons I had learned from my career in counterterrorism and disaster response, a career that began well before September 11, 2001.

So I was at a stoplight, but also a crossroads. Go straight and I would arrive home. Turn right onto Storrow Drive and I would return to CNN, back downtown, where I would analyze and assess the unfolding response to yet another crisis in our homeland. The scenario was disturbingly familiar.

The light turned green, and the way forward was obvious. The homeland could wait.

THE MAKING OF A
TERRORISM EXPERT

I AM A "SECURITY MOM."

The term first went mainstream in the 2004 presidential election, to describe a voting bloc of women who were white, suburban, and with children, and who were really, really worried about terrorism. They didn't do much about it but worry a lot. Did I mention that they worried? Occasionally, when the world was less than stable, they might actually freak out: I have this image of the smart and funny main character in *I Love Lucy* turning into a hapless scaredy-cat when she sees a mouse, and then screaming to her manly husband—"Ricky!"—for protection. These college-educated women—whether single, married, divorced, or widowed—just threw up their hands and cowered like the very children they were so worried about protecting. And despite the fact that this population is usually defined by its natural inclination toward progressive social causes, when it came to the war in Iraq and concern over the war on terror, they largely voted Republican.

It isn't clear whether security moms were actually a deciding factor in the 2004 George W. Bush versus John Kerry presidential election. No matter. The security mom became a cultural and marketing phenomenon. And she was utterly defenseless in an age of terror.

Screw that. We need a new definition.

"Security mom" can and should mean a woman who plans and prepares as she raises her children in a world where anything can happen. Exceptionally rational, a security mom views the yellow sticky note as god's greatest invention since the slow cooker. Whether she works or not, she isn't defenseless, waiting for someone else to protect her. There are security dads too, trust me, and security singles and security partners and security grandparents. The list goes on. They are all out there. They just don't know it.

Yet.

I am not the same person I was in 2001, when terror first struck our homeland so vividly, when those of us already a part of the "terrorism expert" class suddenly became relevant. My thinking about security has changed significantly since then; I have come to realize that a nation too focused on preventing bad things from happening is on a fool's errand. Instead, we should simply, but resourcefully, reclaim our resiliency. I call this "grip"—it's a more active, more in-your-face, more powerful form of resiliency. We prepare, respond, adapt, and then brace for the next thing. We practice these habits of grip. We know that nothing goes according to plan. Sh-t happens: that is the profound knowledge that defines a security mom.

A nation that empowers its citizens with this knowledge becomes a safer nation as a whole. Imagine a nation built around the notion that "sh-t happens," a nation that did not view the often violent jolts to our systems—hurricanes, and oil spills, and terrorists, and viruses, and earthquakes—as abnormal, but as always the possible consequences of living in a globally interconnected society. Imagine if we understood that invulnerability is impossible and instead focused on how to reduce risk and respond to crises when they inevitably happen, with vigor. Imagine if every citizen then felt empowered to implement strategies of preparedness, knowing, as we surely do, that, something, anything could happen.

I am so often asked: "Are we safe?" This question has plagued me for my entire career. It has been asked by family and friends, students and scholars, news anchors and government officials.

The most accurate answer is, "Of course not; what kind of question is that?" But I get why it's asked. Us "real" experts—and you can put whatever descriptor you want in front, whether it be "homeland security," "national security," "terrorism," "aviation," "hurricane," "public health," "military," "crisis"—have too often sold a vision of society that has never existed. Sure, we can be safer, but we can never be *safe*.

We are a homeland like no other—a federal structure with fifty governors, all kings and queens unto themselves; hundreds of cities with transit systems that only function when on time; frantic commercial activity crisscrossing borders on roadways, railways, and airways; the expectation of every working mother that when she orders yet another iPhone 6 charger on Amazon.com, it will arrive the next day; and, oh yes, the desire that our nation not just focus on security but also attend to schools, health care, transportation, civil rights and civil liberties, and every other large and small concern voiced by its citizens. America is built to be unsafe, and thank goodness for that.

Over the years, as terrorist attacks and related incidents grew in frequency—maybe because we called it a "war"—something happened to make the public feel powerless and disinvested in its own safety. The experts, like me, are partially to blame. People in my field uphold a culture of paternalism that has done much to protect the public, but much more to ignore it.

We—meaning the band of homeland security experts that I had been a part of—somehow convinced the public that the responsibility for their security, and the security of this inherently unsafe nation, could be fully delegated. Too many on both sides—the public and the experts—believed it. That belief came with a rising cost: We completely neglected to educate Americans about homeland security. We dismissed Americans' capacity to learn, to engage, to act. As a consequence, the substantive benefits of resiliency were not explained; the habits of grip were not nurtured.

The safety of our nation is dependent on skills that we already practice to keep ourselves and our children safer at home, in our communities. And those of us who work in homeland security failed to disclose this one basic fact: You are a security expert, too. You are familiar with these skills. You know the refrains of every parent: Look both ways, wear your helmet, call when you get there. But rather than building on the practices of security cultivated in nearly every household, homeland security was treated as if it had less and less to do with what happened in our homes. The result was to make us more—not less—vulnerable.

So much ink has been spilled over how we can prevent harm from coming our way. So little has been disclosed about what happens when that harm comes to pass. I can debate until I'm bored with myself about the need for climate mitigation measures, stronger gun control, or a more vigorous public health system. Yes, we live in an age of exceptional danger, but it takes a certain amount of amnesia to believe we are unique in this regard. The truth is we have always been vulnerable. In this sense, homeland security is also much like home security—both are built on the mistakes of the past and forward lessons learned for the future. My own mother likes to remind me, after I leave her with "recommendations" for how to look after my kids when she offers to babysit, that she has some experience in this field. Our mothers learned from theirs, as we surely learn from ours, and as our children will surely learn from us. No generation is particularly exceptional in figuring this out; all we can do is try to avoid making the same mistakes twice.

The warning that keeps sounding, year after year, generation after generation, is this: No government ought to guarantee perfect security, because no government can provide it. There has never been a time of perfect peace. Indeed, there is only one promise that government should make: that it will invest in creating a more resilient nation. And that promise begins with acknowledging that citizens must be a part of this plan. For any society to be more resilient, the public must be briefed. They must assume a certain amount of responsibility for their safety and adopt the habits of grip. We can cross our fingers and hope for the best, but I don't believe in luck—not, at least, as a tactic for safety in the homeland or in my home.

But I wasn't so sure how to relate these messages. How could I explain that we all had the capacity to build more resilient communities, one home at a time, using the same skills we have mastered at home: grip, flexibility, planning, backup plans? Then, in 2011, my cousin Karen wrote me an e-mail. The subject line read: "Al Qaeda."

Karen is a little older than me, with daughters who are already out of college. She is a dentist, and she has, over the years, scolded me for barely flossing. Thankfully, she also gives me great advice for how to address my deteriorating gum situation (see above re: flossing). I try to return the favor when I can.

"Hi Juliette," she began. She continued:

> Can you help? Debbie is in Pennsylvania and she wants to go to NYC for the weekend. But I just saw that they think there could be a ten-year anniversary attack there, so I don't want her to go. She says I am crazy. I said I would contact you. Would you send your kids? By the way, how are your gums? Are you flossing? Don't forget to sleep with your night guard. And let me know about the terrorists.

Dental care and bin Laden: never before have the two been so closely aligned. But there was something illuminating in Karen's questions. She wanted to assume a certain amount of responsibility for her daughter's safety, but she didn't know where to begin. Her e-mail clarified what I had always suspected—there is something missing from our nation's security efforts.

Karen just wanted the lowdown: *Tell me about these scary things, whether they are terrorists, natural disasters, or viruses. Tell me how it works and what I should do to protect my loved ones. Tell me what you would do if it was your child who wanted to travel this weekend. Tell me just like I would tell you about your gums.*

Simply: Bring it home.

I have served at the highest levels of state and federal government in homeland and national security—for one governor, Deval Patrick, and two presidents, Bill Clinton and Barack Obama. I have also raised three children. Their birth years coincide with traumatic events in American history: Cecilia was born in 2001, just a few weeks after we lost three thousand citizens when two planes flew into the World Trade Center in New York, another plane destroyed parts of the Pentagon, and another was lost in the fields of Pennsylvania. Leo arrived in 2003, as US troops, deployed by an administration looking for revenge above anything else, invaded Iraq. Jeremiah came into this world in 2005, soon after Hurricane Katrina, the deadliest hurricane in America's history, devastated the Gulf Coast. Celebration and destruction link my own home with my homeland.

As the governor's homeland security advisor, I oversaw my state's National Guard and, on his behalf, authorized the deployment of troops abroad; I am also a master at the game Battleship, mercilessly mobilizing fleets and defeating my kids. As President Obama's assistant secretary for homeland security, I have done my time in the Situation Room; I have also spent endless hours in local emergency rooms, once after Leo used Jeremiah's head as a football. I have been cleansed in a post–radiation exposure shower after an unfortunate (though thankfully a false-positive test result) experience in a nuclear facility—but I found getting lice out of all my children's hair after an unfortunate sleepover much more debilitating.

I have spent my career protecting my home and homeland, and I want to share what I have learned. My hope is that through these stories, my experiences in the strange and secretive world of homeland security—more maligned than understood—will become accessible to the American public. It is time we made this whole scary, confusing, seemingly idiotic, totally unapproachable apparatus personal. I have simply come to believe that the challenges, conflicts, and choices inherent in protecting the homeland are really not that different from those we encounter every day. The touchstones of protecting both— grip, preparedness, spare capacity, flexibility, communication, learning from the past—are essentially the same.

And with that, I present myself as Exhibit A.

I must first concede that I am an unlikely terrorism expert. I am still consistently surprised that my professional career focuses on violent events, from the threat of terrorism to other, wide-ranging threats including climate change and mass shootings.

I was born and raised in Los Angeles, California, where I spent afternoons and weekends at the beach, playing volleyball and working on my tan. I grew up at a time when skin cancer seemed a remote-enough possibility that my girlfriends and I would slather ourselves in baby oil instead of sunscreen. I dreamed of being a professional volleyball player, a zoologist, a Russian scholar (I dropped that after a short-lived and academically disastrous foray into the language), and then a lawyer. At my all-girls high school, I had teachers with first names like "King" and last names like "Wildflower." It was California in the 1980s.

I am the daughter of an immigrant family—my mother was born

in Lebanon, and my dad's family also came from there, though they would actually meet in a carpool to UCLA, which they both attended as students. My parents prioritized academics, and were strict enough to make me spend one weekend night home with them throughout my high school career. I was a dedicated student, got good grades, played varsity sports, and even spent a summer at debate camp, for which my cooler older sister, Marisa, still teases me. I was eventually accepted at Harvard College, and I moved to Cambridge. Though I have drifted back and forth to DC during Democratic administrations, I have remained in Massachusetts ever since.

Massachusetts is where I met my husband, David, when I was nineteen. I am mortified to admit it was at the Harvard-Yale football game—at the tailgate, no less. It all sounds so predictable, but at that age, we had our ups and downs, breakups and makeups, and ultimately, after attending Harvard Law School together, we moved down to DC to work in the Clinton administration's Justice Department. We rented an apartment, bought IKEA furniture, got married.

I was twenty-six when I made my initial foray into government. My first legal job had nothing to do with security in the traditional sense. In 1995, I began as an attorney in the Civil Rights Division of the Department of Justice. Assistant Attorney General Deval Patrick was my boss; Janet Reno was attorney general. I flew around the country on behalf of the federal government litigating for the protection of citizens' rights, mostly in schools. While I worked on long-standing desegregation cases—from St. Louis to Mississippi—I also contributed to more novel litigation, including opening up the Citadel and the Virginia Military Institute to female cadets. I was allowed to initiate the federal government's first peer-on-peer violence (what we now call "bullying") case against a California school district that turned a blind eye toward its football team's behavior. Previously, civil rights cases had only been brought against school districts that directly violated students' rights. In this case, I determined that a federal civil rights action could be initiated against a school district that failed to protect students from other students. The district eventually settled, and instituted tougher rules to protect female students from the physical and verbal harassment of its football team.

I loved my job. I loved my husband. Essentially, I loved our life. I thought my future would unfold rather predictably: I would spend my career championing civil rights and working for the progressive causes that had inspired me to attend law school in the first place. It didn't. I soon learned, as I explained above, that nothing goes according to plan. Sh-t happens.

On April 19, 1995, just a few months before I began at the Justice Department, Timothy McVeigh and his cohorts bombed Oklahoma City's Alfred P. Murrah Federal Building, killing 168 people and injuring another 300. This was homegrown terrorism, but it furthered a slow awakening, initiated after the first terrorist attack on the World Trade Center in 1993, of our vulnerabilities at home. Because the issues surrounding McVeigh's actions were politically difficult to address—right-wing extremism, domestic radicalization, gun control—in the aftermath of that tragedy, Congress deflected and passed the Omnibus Counterterrorism Act of 1995, which addressed immigration and foreign terrorism instead.

The act gave the FBI the power to detain non–US

citizens indefinitely, even if they were here lawfully, based on secret evidence—evidence so secret that it would not be disclosed to the defendant in a court of law. In the years after it was passed, the number of terrorists charged under the act was relatively small: A dozen men, all Muslim and all from Arab countries, were detained without the opportunity to refute the evidence against them. Because they were not US citizens, the argument held, they did not have the same Fifth Amendment right to cross-examination that a US citizen would have. These prosecutions came to be known as the "secret evidence" cases.

One case highlighted the ease with which the legislation's flawed logic could be exploited. The judge—the only party besides the prosecutors authorized to see the "secret evidence"—disclosed in ruling against the United States that the highly classified "smoking gun" in the case consisted of testimony by the man's ex-wife. The judge ruled that the wife, surely aware that accusing her husband of terrorism would earn her full custody of their children, was not a reliable source as to her husband's "terrorist" status.

As more and more judges exposed the errors of these prosecutions, Attorney General Janet Reno intervened. After all, these were all federal cases, and the US attorneys who built (and lost) these cases reported to her. Arab and Muslim political groups, such as the Arab American Institute and the American Muslim Political Action Committee, publicly criticized the act; they met with Reno several times during the latter part of Clinton's second term. Reno sympathized with their complaints. She had spent her professional career in a courtroom where an open, if adversarial, spirit reigned; this particular use of classified information challenged her legacy. By 1998, Reno decided to exercise her tremendous authority to investigate the consequences of this piece of legislation, mainly in her own department.

By then, I had contributed to some high-profile cases as a civil rights litigator and line attorney at the Justice Department. I was also, incidentally, the only high-ranking Arab-American at the Justice Department when Reno turned her attention to the Omnibus Counterterrorism Act. She asked me to join her daily 8:15 a.m. all-hands meeting, where her senior team convened to discuss a range of litigation activities— from anti-trust to civil rights to environmental protection. I regularly arrived a few minutes late, with wet hair (at twenty-nine and with no kids, 8:15 a.m. seemed early to break out the blow-dryer).

Reno put me on a team charged with reviewing the "secret evidence" cases. We examined how the FBI investigated these individuals, and whether these actions constituted a proper use of its authority. I would sit in a room secured for classified information with colleagues from the national security apparatus, poring over the files of these cases. Our mandate was to declassify as much material as possible and to determine whether the cases were actually legitimate exercises of governmental authority. My background in civil rights law proved immediately helpful. Most civil rights cases, after all, are brought against government entities such as housing authorities or police departments or, as was true of the "secret evidence" cases, the FBI.

That review appointment made two things clear. First, as an Arab-American who now had an intimate understanding of the complex legal and operational issues surrounding our national security, I could act as a bridge between groups such as the Arab American

Institute and the American Muslim Political Action Committee and the government. The Arab-American community was starting to organize, and they sought increased access to government officials to press their agenda on a variety of topics, including Middle East peace, civil rights, and hate crime legislation. While I did not professionally identify as Arab-American, nor did I work with or for the political groups clamoring for recognition, I had the right heritage and the right credentials for this role.

Second, I was becoming a "terrorism expert." As my work drew me deeper into the national security apparatus, I became privy to information about the threats to our nation from various terrorist organizations thriving abroad and at home, as well as about the amount of activity—surveillance, intelligence operations, military actions, law enforcement raids—being performed to protect the country.

At first, it was hard for me to reconcile these new roles with the career trajectory I had once imagined. I'd spent hours in law school defending prisoners in administrative hearings against corrections officers. I'd spent the summer after my first year in law school in Montgomery, Alabama, working on death penalty appeals for lawyer and *Just Mercy: A Story of Justice and Redemption* author Bryan Stevenson. I boarded at the home of Virginia Durr, the white activist who helped bail out Rosa Parks after she was arrested on that bus in 1955. Indeed, the first time I encountered anything related to terrorism was outside the office. The "Unabomber," Ted Kaczynski, had added my scientist brother, Jon Faiz Kayyem, to a list of potential targets, and, after Kaczynski's arrest in 1996, the government wanted to make sure there were no unopened boxes around his house.

I was not born to be a terrorism expert. I simply morphed into one, in stages.

Stage One: Admission. Literally.

I applied for and was eventually granted top-secret security clearance. This wasn't a test of academic prowess or firearms acumen or language skills. It was a lot of forms—a series of questions to be answered under penalty of perjury. Some of these were tedious: I had to list all places of residence for the last fifteen years. Others were simply silly: I had to swear that I had never supported the Communist Party or advocated the downfall of the United States.

Only one made me groan, and then laugh: I had to list my foreign-born relatives. My mother, born Milly Deeb, has eight brothers and sisters. As I wrote down the birthplaces of my aunts and uncles, I traced my family's path to America:

Eddie	Kooba, Lebanon (in the Batroun District)
Alice	Havana, Cuba
Libby	Kooba, Lebanon
Carrie	Kooba, Lebanon
Milly (my mother)	Kooba, Lebanon
Rosie	Kentucky, United States
George	Kentucky, United States
Janice	Kentucky, United States
Georgette	Kentucky, United States

This list still cracks me up. It looks so nefarious without context. I imagined a distraught FBI agent reading my clearance papers, trying to piece together the strange journey that led my family from Lebanon to Cuba, back again to Lebanon, and finally to Kentucky.

I was asked, predictably, for more information. So began a seemingly endless back-and-forth about my family's exodus so many decades ago. The men and women charged with granting security clearance needed proof of my statements on the form. So I obliged: old passports, documents, aged papers from decades past, notarized written statements when nothing else could be found. Even when I thought I was done, I received requests for more proof: travel logs, social security numbers, records of foreign business interests, marriage certificates, and driver's licenses. And once wasn't enough. Security clearances are regularly updated, and as I rose in the government over the years, the reviews became more rigorous—proof, more proof, and even more proof.

My mother's mother, Rose—or, as I called her, Situ, which means "grandmother" in some dialects of Arabic—and my grandfather were young and poor when they left Lebanon for the first time in 1929. They traveled to Cuba, hoping to make their way to America after two previous attempts had been thwarted. Before Castro assumed power, Cuba promised easy access to America for immigrants in search of a better life. Notices in newspapers throughout the developing world lured adventure seekers to Cuban shores, advertising a pit stop on the way to the Promised Land. It turned out this was a ruse; access to the United States was no easier from Cuba than it was from Lebanon. My grandparents stayed in Havana long enough for my grandmother to give birth to their second child. Older now but still poor, and with no family in Cuba, they returned to Lebanon in 1932. They would stay there long enough to welcome three more children, including my mother.

My mother was their last child born in Kooba, a small mountain village where neighbors greeted guests for tea with a selection of fresh mints and a range of cigarette boxes. Their house was the size of a few parking spaces. (In fact, when I visited years later, it actually had been demolished to build two parking spaces.) When my mother was just one, the family accomplished from Lebanon what they couldn't from Cuba and, with papers in hand, arrived at Ellis Island.

Or at least, this is what I thought for most of my life. The myths immigrant families create to explain their journeys to new lands cannot be easily verified. My mother and her family had always told one story, which culminated in their arrival on the great island that had welcomed so many before them. Had we scrutinized further, we would have noticed that Situ's documents showed a different route through the port of New York. The ruse was discovered not by the enterprising FBI agent who pored over my clearance papers but by a curious uncle fascinated with the family tree.

Here's the kicker: Situ lived a long time, and she must have known that we were all perpetuating the Ellis Island lie. Her journey from Lebanon to Cuba to America was a source of great pride. She had overcome countless obstacles to bring her family here. My grandparents belonged to a generation of immigrants that became Americans, and their supposed arrival on Ellis Island was an important signifier of that new identity. So I can understand why she might not have been inclined to correct this mistake. It also made for a great story.

I know, for a fact, that the next part of that great story is true: The Deebs settled in Kentucky, where the weather was appealing. Kentucky is horse country, which must have felt familiar to so many Arabs who raised and groomed these animals before arriving in America. The Deebs did not last long in Kentucky—nor did my grandparents' marriage. I can only imagine how bad their relationship became, for Situ willingly divorced my grandfather and raised nine children on her own. No one speaks of Eli, my grandfather. I have never seen a picture of him. He holds no place in my head or my heart, and years later, when David and I proposed to name our second son Eli because we liked the name, I was surprised when my mother looked at me fiercely and said "You will not name him that." I had forgotten about my grandfather. We were taught to look forward, not back.

Like so many others, the Deebs went west. Situ had had her first child at age fourteen; the age difference between her and her eldest son, Edward, was ten years less than the age difference between her eldest and her youngest child. She is remembered by more than one hundred children, grandchildren, and great-grandchildren. ("Juliette who?" I am sometimes asked when I attend a crowded family event in Los Angeles. "Oh, you're Milly's youngest.")

There is, of course, another side to my family: the Kayyems. I was also required to produce proof of *their* journey to America. My paternal grandfather, Faiz, was born in Lebanon (or possibly some part of Syria), and married my grandmother, also named Rose, a much younger beauty. The exact nature of his business varied; he was in textiles from Japan, silk from China, real estate in Hawaii. He was, by all accounts, successful, if not impatient. He moved his family into nine different rental homes, requiring my dad to attend eight different schools by the time he graduated high school. My dad was raised in Hawaii and California, where he would eventually meet my mother.

My parents may have come from the same corner of the world, but they were raised under very different circumstances.

Strict and domineering, Faiz roused a rebellious spirit in my dad that has animated him for his entire life. Consider, as I did while filling out those forms, the notorious story of my father's arrest. As a college student, he was once accused of robbery and assault on a policeman. The charge was unsubstantiated and soon dismissed after he was held for two days—it turns out my dad had lost his wallet close to the scene of the crime. But this episode engendered a lasting habit among all Kayyems: we are skeptical of first reports (in my dark-haired dad's case, the assailant was described as "redheaded"), a legacy that has served me well throughout my career. My father's childhood boasted other incidents that proved of little interest with regard to my security clearance, thankfully. There were fistfights in Catholic schools; more than one near-death experience in the ocean around Hawaii; and pictures of him from the 1970s with a moustache, large collars, and cigarettes (before he and my mother embraced the healthy lifestyle that makes them very youthful seventy-plus-year-olds today). Simply put, my dad knew how to have fun, in his own way. One time, as an experiment, my dad tried to fit my older brother, Jon Faiz; my sister, Marisa; and me on his Harley Davidson for a ride around West Los Angeles. The experiment worked, but then he had to face my mother.

As I finished the last question on those painfully long forms, I was actually thankful for the opportunity to retrace my family's journeys. It was a way to acknowledge how the Kayyem and Deeb histories have shaped my professional beliefs. My ancestors lived in a country with a long and painful legacy of civil war, and I grew up listening to stories that taught me people are more resilient than we might expect. My opposition to the 2003 Iraq War grew from my knowledge of Lebanon's sad history of occupation. I spent many dinners with Arabs who could have told the war's planners not to expect roses in the streets of Baghdad, and I listened. I support comprehensive immigration reform because I recognize how this nation thrives when it welcomes those who wish to immigrate. Not so long ago, my family chose this country as their home. I have seen the statistics and I believe profiling is ineffective at best, unlawful at worst. I have also seen how many people are profiled—like my brother, Jon Faiz, when he is unshaven. I take issue with the NYPD's nicely named "Demographics Unit," which targeted Muslim and Arab communities. It was an unsuccessful program. I knew it would be, because I know—from Situ's experience—that America's greatest strength is its acceptance of all religions and creeds.

When I turned in my completed forms, I sat down with the FBI agent to discuss my security clearance. He had already interviewed my friends, neighbors, and family, who had doubly validated my claims. The agent congratulated me. "Welcome to the club," he said.

It didn't feel like true acceptance—more like my proof had held up, for now. The vagaries of my security clearance review, the journey it unearthed, meant that I would always feel that I had one foot firmly in the security world, but that the other lingered behind, tethered to my history, my background, my identity, my family, my home. I didn't know it then, but I would spend the rest of my career trying to become someone who could fit into all these worlds: the daughter of an immigrant family, an East Coast transplant from California, a young bride to her college sweetheart, a public servant, a security expert, and, eventually, a mother.

THE DAYS BEFORE

IN 1995, WHEN I WAS TWENTY-SIX AND DAVID WAS TWENTY-EIGHT, WE MOVED to Washington, DC, to work in the Clinton administration. We lived on the second floor of a narrow town house in Adams Morgan, a neighborhood in the northwest part of the city. We paid dirt-cheap rent for a place that felt that way. Our landlord, Sam, would fix the leak in our sink, but it often meant that a new leak would emerge in our shower. We were childless, but it seemed like we were always busy. My starting salary was less than a third of what my peers made at law firms; we didn't save a penny, preferring to spend it on our social life, meeting friends at bars for late-night get-togethers throughout the late first and early second terms of the Clinton administration. We were all fearless and in debt. Our first-floor neighbors worked to save the world through nonprofit organizations and, when the world didn't respond, smoked more pot than we thought was possible, the smell wafting into our closet through a big hole in the floor. Our upstairs neighbor would later become the chief of staff to the CIA director, and while he agreed to water our plants when we were out of town, he kept his distance. My friend, who had a crush on him, used to giggle when we passed him on the steps of the house. "Do you think he's killed people with his bare hands?" she'd whisper.

By 1998, as I was approaching the magical age of thirty, I had left the courtroom to become counsel to the assistant attorney general for civil rights, Bill Lann Lee. I now dealt exclusively with policy issues surrounding the Justice Department's civil-rights strategy. These covered a range of topics from the ongoing review of the "secret evidence" cases to Attorney General Reno's decision to reopen the Martin Luther King, Jr. assassination investigation, from police brutality at the NYPD to the "mend it, don't end it" reform of affirmative action. I spent a lot more time in DC than on the road, on Capitol Hill, or at the White House. I could have stayed in the city forever. I was in no hurry to leave. It was the beginning of my lifelong love for government service, for trying to make government work.

David's office was down two flights of stairs and a couple of massive hallways away from mine, on the fifth floor of the building known as "Main Justice." He worked as an attorney in the Office of Legal Counsel (OLC), which provided the While House with legal advice about executive-branch conduct. The office would, later on, become famous as the place where attorney John Yoo drafted the "torture memos" that provided the Bush administration a legal justification for waterboarding and other brutal interrogation methods. But during the

Clinton years, the office wasn't too much in the news. David, a former Supreme Court clerk and law review editor, was a perfect fit for OLC. He provided rigorous legal analysis to the White House and spent his spare time writing law journal articles, in anticipation of becoming a law professor one day. As he wrote, I trained for my first marathons. While he researched the legal writings of a nineteenth-century scholar named Thomas M. Cooley, I researched new paths along the Rock Creek Parkway, across the Potomac, and through Virginia to get my mileage up. When I ran the New York City Marathon for the first time, David cheered for me at Mile 6, had brunch with friends, then met me at the finish line. He liked the distribution of duties.

In the spring of 1999, several offers to teach law came in for David. I knew when we got married that this moment would come: I would have to play the faculty spouse as deans tried to lure my husband to their school. I often felt miscast in the role: I found the formalities of academic dinner parties insufferable. I was too often asked what I thought of Tom Friedman's latest article. I found the conversation, when not predictable, disheartening. "I'm surprised," I remember hearing a professor say about a former student who had just won a very big, public case, "because he wasn't on the law review." Life, I knew, didn't begin and end with the law review.

If I'm being somewhat unkind, please know it is only because I was an exceptionally average student in law school. I didn't like it very much. While David served on the law review, I avoided class-work and interned for public service efforts, like prisoners' rights advocacy and death penalty appeals. I was never very inclined to speak to a law professor, and now I found myself married to one.

The offers came from schools across the nation, and David stewed as if he had a choice. Of course, he did have a choice, but he then would have had to deal with my mother. Harvard Law had welcomed him back, this time as faculty. My mother—exposing some of the immigrant attitude that was clearly part of her makeup—called our house.

"Can he actually say no?" she asked me, in all seriousness.

"Yes, Mom," I said. "He has free will."

"It would just be so hard to explain why he didn't accept the offer now that I've told just about everyone in the family," she said.

He did say yes. And so I followed. Looking back at my career, I have struggled with that verb, but "followed" seems about right. Women like me are so often told that we have to master our own destiny; "followed" doesn't fit into the narrative. But sometimes that destiny demands we take a leap of tremendous faith. "Followed" isn't a criticism, nor is it an apology. It's a choice, too.

We started to look for houses in Cambridge in 1999. I began to close out my legal projects, handing them to the next eager lawyer. I had no job in Cambridge, so Attorney General Reno looked out for me: She asked me to continue my work on the "secret evidence" cases. The project was coming to a close in any event, so we devised a plan where I would come back periodically to Main Justice to assist with the oversight. That offer was a lifeline. I had no employment prospects in Massachusetts. I was about to give up an important job, and felt like I was losing my identity. Attorney General Reno gave me a little reprieve.

We drove our own U-Haul north and settled into our new town

house (this time all ours) in Porter Square, just a mile from David's job at Harvard and only slightly farther from where David and I first met. The town house was narrow but stood four stories high; it never crossed my mind then that this would, one day, mean carrying sleepy children up many flights of stairs. I decorated and painted the square rooms. We finally bought a new car. We settled in for the long haul.

But I was bored as hell. David headed into his office, and I took up a variety of hobbies—mountain biking, yoga, even knitting—to fill the hours. I surprised David by bringing home a puppy; he didn't seem too anxious about the fact that I had done so without any planning whatsoever. We talked about starting a family, but my professional life seemed so in flux that I worried I would lose whatever momentum I had built. The dog, a Labrador mix from the pound, seemed enough for now. We named her Scout.

During that leisurely summer of 1999, I didn't realize that a series of events unfolding around the world would soon launch me on the next phase of my career path. The year before, a radical terrorist, unknown to most, had planned and executed simultaneous attacks on two US embassies in Africa. Most of those killed were Africans, but the attacks exposed America's vulnerability in the face of an asymmetric threat, one that was dangerous because of its small size, its secretive nature, its leanness. This was a different kind of terrorism. In historical context, it was commonly understood that terrorist organizations planned attacks that would be public, with a lot of people watching, but not too deadly, for fear that their cause would be labeled as sociopathic rather than political. Terrorists didn't want to kill a lot of people; they just wanted to make a point.

This Al Qaeda group was different. There were no traditional demands, such as the release of prisoners. Instead, this group wanted America to end its military involvement in the Middle East, to stop its citizens from being so loose and immoral, to recede, to simply not exist. Later federal prosecutions of the main perpetrators of the bombings showed that their Saudi Arabian–born leader was heavily involved in the planning of the embassy attacks, at one stage even suggesting that a car bomb detonate on the opposite side of the entrance than had previously been proposed. He was tactical and engaged, and his group—veterans from the Afghan war against Russia—was tightly knit. He found a safe haven in Afghanistan.

Osama bin Laden represented a new kind of threat. The US government was not structured to address his attacks easily: the State Department bureaus concentrated on different regions of the world; the Defense Department featured a command structure—Pacific or Asian Command—that mirrored resources and military planning; the intelligence agencies were similarly focused on nation-states and the espionage that occurs between them; and the Justice Department lawyers prosecuted terror cases in the courtroom, rendering punishment that came in handy only after an attack. Counterterrorism needed a home, and there wasn't one to speak of.

In this vacuum, or maybe because of it, in 1999, Congress created the National Commission on Terrorism to assess the growing global threat and to make nonbinding recommendations regarding America's response and preparedness. I was wise enough to know that a congressional commission wields about as much clout as did the city of Cambridge when it decided to become a "non-nuclear zone"; it is often a way for leaders to punt on an issue, drown it in delay, and then take the recommendations under advisement to die an anonymous death.

By statute, the commission would have ten members: five Democrats and five Republicans. Nine were picked without much controversy, among them people who would later become leaders of the post-9/11 "war on terror" during the Bush administration. Its chairman was L. Paul Bremer, who, as the first head of the US Coalition Provisional Authority in Iraq, disbanded the Iraqi army against the wishes of America's military leaders, resulting in years of armed resistance. The commission's other members included General Wayne Downing, whose vision for a lean, "get in, get out" military effort in Iraq was ignored but whose legacy was evidenced in the raid on bin Laden's compound over a decade later; Clinton's former head of the CIA, Jim Woolsey, who had no love for his former boss and who viewed America's intelligence efforts as severely neglected; and Jane Harman, a once and future Democratic congresswoman from California who would be a vocal member of the House Intelligence Committee through much of the war on terror. This was no lightweight group of experts. What's more, each was sufficiently free from government service at that moment to offer an honest assessment of how America could best address the threat.

But the tenth commissioner proved to be an issue. He was a Muslim American named Salam Al-Marayati, an activist from Los Angeles who was identified, and self-identified, not so much as a terrorism expert but as someone who reflected the concerns and understanding of the American Muslim community. Conservative groups roundly condemned his nomination, and the Zionist Organization of America launched a vicious campaign against Al-Marayati after it was discovered that he had compared some of Israel's ardent supporters to Adolf Hitler. Al-Marayati's life's work in promoting interfaith dialogue was reduced to a debate over a few words. The fight over his appointment was political, and religious, and ugly.

The story made for explosive headlines in newspapers as it pitted Arabs and Jews and Republicans and Democrats all against one another. The House minority leader, Richard Gephardt, who had appointed Al-Marayati, harbored higher aspirations after his failed presidential bid in 1988 and needed—desperately—to get rid of the problem without seeming to acquiesce to the mob. So he came up with an excuse: Al-Marayati couldn't get a security clearance fast enough to meet the commission's statutory deadlines. It was likely true, given the nature of the clearance process I knew all too well, one that is onerous for anybody with a name like Al-Marayati (or Kayyem, for that matter). But the explanation was also very convenient.

News of Al-Marayati's withdrawn nomination broke on a slow summer morning. David and I were reading the paper together in our new place, a no-kids luxury we took for granted. He was headed to work, and I was scheduled to have several "informational interviews"—a euphemism, I knew, for meetings about jobs that didn't exist at places I wasn't even sure I wanted to work. I was planning on going for a bike ride along the Charles River and maybe periodically complaining to Scout about how David had created these circumstances for me. Here I was: jobless and talking to the dog.

My father called about the Al-Marayati controversy. I knew

many of the key players from my involvement in the review of the "secret evidence" cases. He wanted to know what I thought. I said it all seemed too vicious; Al-Marayati was a committed public advocate, and it looked like the Democrats were in a bind.

"What they need is an Arab Christian with security clearance; that would make everyone equally happy," he said, ominously.

Three days later, as I was leaving a yoga class in Cambridge, Gephardt's office called. I eventually met with him and his staff during a hastily convened trip to DC. I satisfied their requirements: I was an acceptable Arab, a terrorism "expert," precleared, and a woman. Within a week, the National Commission on Terrorism put me forward as the new appointee. To this day, I do not know how Gephardt found me. I suspect Janet Reno had something to do with it, but I have to admit that for a long time I wondered if my father had figured out a way to contact Gephardt directly.

The announcement, and the continuing controversy over the commission, led to a *New York Times* story about my new position. Within the first few paragraphs—after discussing my background, and the fact that I was Christian and not Muslim—it mentioned that I was married to a Jewish lawyer. This was a fact I never conveyed to the reporter, but suspect that others offered up. The Democrats needed to show that I was a safe appointment, qualified and also acceptable to all of the religious, political, and ethnic groups invested in the issue: a Christian Arab-American terrorist expert born in California and married to a Jewish law professor—a Harvard law professor, no less! I understood the drill. Nonetheless, Situ called me, angry. The *Times* headline had read, "Arab-American Appointed to

Commission on Terrorism." "You tell them," she said, "that you are not Arab, you are Lebanese." My people can be as parochial as the best of them.

And so, I kind of found a job. Or, more accurately, a job found me. For almost a year, I commuted to DC to meet regularly with the commission in a nondescript building owned by the CIA. We traveled to the Middle East and Europe. Our staff included people whom we addressed by generic names like "Robin" and "Sam," though they were CIA operatives whose real names were known only to their mothers. We heard evidence from experts and analysts, from government officials, and even from journalists. We heard from those who had been tracking bin Laden for years, and others who thought our time and resources should be directed elsewhere. We heard about how America's public safety apparatus was wholly unprepared for a domestic attack, as our civil defense structures had waned since the Cold War. Tellingly—despite what was argued years later, after 9/11—we never heard that Iraq was a threat, nor was that country ever mentioned in our final report. At my insistence, because of my experience, the commission did recommend ending the use of secret evidence in cases in federal court, recognizing that open and adversarial proceedings were better suited for these kinds of prosecutions. I got to complete the task that Reno had charged me with so many years before.

While Bremer was adamant about the commissioners agreeing, unanimously, on all findings in the report, I dug in on an issue that meant a lot to me as a civil rights attorney. I ended up being the sole dissenter on this one policy. This was in spite of the arguments of the Republican commissioners, who, as the 2000 election approached, knew that the report, sometimes critical of the Clinton administration, could land in the midst of a contentious presidential battle. The commission recommended loosening some of the traditional legal barriers to intelligence sharing within law enforcement, arguing that this change would make it easier for us to "connect the dots." It sounded right on paper, perhaps, but such a wholesale departure from the legal norms of surveillance in the United States and of US citizens abroad required more than just a brief mention. As a lawyer in the field, I knew that the laws were not the reason why our intelligence agencies had failed to address a growing threat. Blaming the law is always an easy excuse—especially for nonlawyers. The real problem was that we had so little good intelligence to speak of.

If we worried that the report, released later in June 2000, would find its way to the wastebasket early, one recommendation ensured that it would be newsworthy. It had become clear to us that the United States simply had no plan to deal with a major terrorist crisis—no sense of who would take charge, and no clear rules for the deployment of the military should a situation require it. The military has tremendous resources available to a governor, in his or her capacity as commander in chief of a state's National Guard, or a president, in an emergency situation, but no law outlined its potential, or eventual, use domestically. Because we are a democracy, with civilian control over the military, a president is not allowed to command its domestic use absent a really, really big-deal event—say, an insurrection. Given that standard, we recommended that the military, in the event of a major terrorist attack, be fully integrated into America's response planning and even, if the situation required it, be the leader of response efforts should local efforts fail. The report was immediately perceived as warmongering.

Nick, an old colleague of mine from the Justice Department, called. He couldn't curb his laughter as he remarked that I was long gone from civil rights litigation. The commission was being described as a right-wing group of paranoids. Only one network was taking us seriously. "Well, at least Fox News likes you," Nick remarked. "To think I knew you when you were a commie."

Headlines and scathing editorials condemned the commission's focus on military efforts. The *New York Times* and the *New Republic*, journals that would later be implicated for their contributions to supporting the war in Iraq, made similar claims: the limited threat to our homeland did not require the kind of military planning for which the commission had asked.

I was required to appear on several news programs and meet with several journals to defend the report. It was my first real introduction to how difficult it is to explain national security to the American public with any precision. Nuance is difficult; we are a nation prone to wild swings in one direction or the other depending on our perception of a threat. At that time, the nation appeared invulnerable.

The commission wasn't my only terrorism-related project at the time, as my appointment led to other opportunities in the field. As Nick suggested, I was on a new trajectory. Immediately after my appointment, law professor and former deputy attorney general Phil Heymann, a man whom I barely knew when I was a student but who fast became a mentor, mentioned that he knew a program at the John

F. Kennedy School of Government at Harvard was looking into the same issues. Richard Falkenrath, a terrorism expert who would later serve as George W. Bush's homeland security advisor, was a young faculty member there. Phil made the introduction. Rich and I met in the fall of 1999, and while our politics were different, our sense of America's vulnerabilities was the same. He asked if I would join his program on domestic preparedness as a research fellow.

In university jargon, a fellow is an academic who is visiting a different institution, a young graduate student who is finishing a PhD, or, as in my case, someone who simply didn't fit into either category. I got paid $2,000 a month for the fellowship. It wasn't nothing, but as a lawyer whose peers were just now landing partnerships at big law firms, I was left with doubts about my professional trajectory. With the commission still meeting several times a month, I was grateful for the fellowship, which gave me an institutional base and a salary in Massachusetts, as well as the freedom to travel and complete my work in DC.

My fellowship at the Kennedy School of Government shaped my thinking about what kind of nation we ought to be in the face of domestic threats. I met a few of those who worked tirelessly in this neglected field. The program gathered leaders in government and the first-responder community to discuss best practices and lessons learned in domestic preparedness efforts. Those two words, "domestic preparedness," would later come to be referred to as "homeland security." With Arnold Howitt, a scholar of local and state government, Falkenrath and the team invited police and fire chiefs, emergency management heads, public health preparedness leaders,

National Guard generals, and others to meet and make tactical rec-ommendations about what America should do in the event of a major attack. While the commission and the domestic preparedness pro-gram held the same view—we were unprepared—only the latter made on-the-ground recommendations for improving our prepared-ness efforts. These included greater focus on ensuring the possibil-ity of radio communication between different organizations during a crisis, stronger alignment of interdisciplinary planning between these departments, from the military to public health, for events that would cross all boundaries, and yes, better integration of military response efforts should civilian efforts fail.

Then Falkenrath left to join the Bush transition team in late 2000, as Vice President Al Gore finally conceded the election. I became co-lead of the program with Howitt as we pursued studies of our homeland defenses and the limitations of our public safety capacity. And through papers and books and training, in a small way, we tried to work with the first-responder community on fortifying our pre-paredness efforts.

What I learned then was that while terms like "domestic pre-paredness" and "homeland security" seemed relatively new, this na-tion has always been figuring out how best to protect itself. After all, we were born from a revolutionary war and suffered through a civil war. From George Washington on, not a single president has been immune to the question of how to protect the homeland. From the beginning, well before 9/11, homeland security has been a work in progress. There has never been a time when we've mastered the bal-ance; the challenge has been a persistent struggle.

And while the Revolutionary and Civil Wars were physically fought in the homeland, it really wasn't until World War I that the notion that civilians—as compared to combatants—could be the targets of a foreign attack began to animate governmental response. World War I gave rise to the awareness that civilians needed to prepare for a new type of warfare, as the Germans opened up a new front with aerial bombardments in France, Belgium, Poland, and eventually England. America, shielded from the direct impact of the First World War, couldn't be so confident in the run-up to the second. As early as 1933, as Hitler made ever clearer his intentions to start a worldwide war, President Franklin Roosevelt was compelled to establish the National Emergency Council. The first of its kind, the council was designed to address and coordinate emergency programs throughout the federal government. It was only a matter of time, many believed, before America would be attacked.

As war raged abroad, and still a year before Pearl Harbor, in a 1940 letter to the president, New York mayor Fiorello La Guardia, echoing the fears of many urban leaders, demanded that the federal government do more than just "coordinate." It needed to "initiate and get things going. Please bear in mind," he wrote to Roosevelt, "that up to this war and never in our history, has the civilian population been exposed to attack."

La Guardia demanded a series of protective services that could help the American public: sirens, bunkers, and evacuation planning. He wanted the federal government to support the equivalent of neighborhood militias. Social-welfare programs, like community engagement and volunteer efforts, were also part of the equation, but

La Guardia viewed the latter as "sissy stuff." While no one today would use that term, La Guardia's point feels familiar: We had to get tough, muscular, and masculine.

Even as Roosevelt acceded to La Guardia's demands, he wasn't convinced that community and volunteer efforts should be abandoned. Roosevelt designated First Lady Eleanor Roosevelt as the symbolic leader of volunteer—mainly Red Cross—activities. Her goal was to engage mothers, daughter, wives, and aunts to support our security efforts, efforts that included the largest intake of women into the labor force in America's history. The two leaders, La Guardia and the first lady, were in constant conflict—the manly versus the sissy, the boy versus the girl.

It was a battle between, for want of better words, the "La Guardias" and the "Eleanors." This tension was as much about personality (or, for that matter, gender) as it was about philosophy. As the war continued, both the mayor and the first lady came to understand the necessity of the other's efforts; a strong civil defense effort had to combine both bunkers and social welfare to best protect the public. And that meant that, eventually, La Guardia and Eleanor would mend fences. But a conceptual divide was there from the start, a divide that persists today. As the Cold War began, world events, budget priorities, and even science and technology would have an impact on chosen policies across the La Guardia/Eleanor spectrum.

By the end of 1945, President Truman had placed most preparedness planning under the supervision of the Department of Defense, but then, fearing a "garrison state," reassigned that effort to a civilian agency. That organization, the National Security Resources Board, was faced with a series of unhappy, but somewhat familiar, questions: In the nuclear age, what level of safety is enough, and how can it be measured? How much "self-help" could the government ask of Americans? How could the message be delivered without terrifying everyone?

Enter *Duck and Cover*, one of nine different preparedness films made after World War II. Bert, a two-foot green cartoon turtle who looks a lot like the landlord in *Three's Company*, is the main character in the film and demonstrates to children how best to survive a nuclear attack should they see the "flash of an atomic bomb." Watching the movie today is a strange trip to an alternate universe where bobby-socked girls and crew-cut boys see a burst of light and fly under their desks. Still, it was applauded at the time as a comforting movie for schoolchildren, despite the fact that experts knew that even a well-timed duck-and-cover was not likely to help most people in a nuclear attack. Nonetheless, the duck-and-cover was practiced by millions of children; it was the most extensive public education campaign of the entire Cold War era.

As the nuclear arms race continued on, and with it existential threats against the American way of life, all of Truman's successors contended with the question of what constituted an appropriate level of civil defense. President Eisenhower, for example, focused on mass evacuation planning, as compared to "duck and cover"; he was responding to the fact that, in 1953, the Russians had tested a hydrogen bomb whose destructive powers were so great that no American city was likely to survive its deployment. Well before the Cuban Missile Crisis brought the world to the brink of nuclear war,

President Kennedy had shifted preparedness efforts toward building community-sheltering capacity. This, in turn, was rendered moot by the notion of "MAD," or mutually assured destruction: By the mid-1960s, the extent of the world's nuclear arsenals had reached a point that any use of them guaranteed the utter destruction of everyone. The power of the weapons themselves was now the sole deterrent to their use. This led President Johnson to abandon all "soft" efforts at civil defense and focus instead on anti–ballistic missile systems.

Given the nature of his undoing, it is too often forgotten that throughout President Nixon's term in office, he faced numerous natural-disaster emergencies, including more than two hundred deaths in the wake of Hurricane Camille along the Mississippi River in 1969. For the first time in history, he permitted funds allocated to preparedness for nuclear attacks to be used for harms brought by Mother Nature, an approach known as "dual-use" planning. Under dual use, whatever gear was in place to deal with a national security threat had to be viable for natural disasters, too.

Dual-use equipment, in the nuclear age, was a revolutionary thought. Nixon had inherited a civilian emergency-preparedness apparatus that was geared toward nuclear war only; his administration then promptly confronted a string of natural disasters. By authorizing the use of funds for dual-use equipment and purchases, he ensured that plans in place to protect American citizens would be viable for national security threats, natural disasters, or any other mayhem. States and localities also favored this approach, knowing that an exclusive focus on foreign threats was expensive and rarely tailored to their specific needs.

Dual-use planning has the benefit of being both efficient and realistic. Think of it as a kind of Band-Aid: you don't really care why your child is bleeding, you only want to deal with the injury. The firefighter who shows up at a burning building does not care, at that moment, whether a terrorist or an arsonist or a careless cigarette smoker is to blame. She just wants to put out the fire as quickly as possible with a hose that works.

Despite these reforms, both Presidents Ford and Carter were left with an inefficient federal disaster-management apparatus. This truth was exposed during the confused response to the nuclear meltdown at Three Mile Island in 1979 in Harrisburg, Pennsylvania—a meltdown caused by a combination of equipment error, faulty design, and worker mistakes. For the first time in US history, an unknown amount of radioactive gas was released into the air. Still, the Carter administration wasn't notified for several hours, and assessment of the harm was imprecise, resulting in Pennsylvania governor Richard Thornburgh's demand for only a partial evacuation of surrounding areas, creating a panic in neighborhoods told to stay put. The recognition that no single federal agency was designated to take charge of the relief effort finally compelled Carter to create an entity solely focused on that task: the Federal Emergency Management Agency (FEMA).

Carter's Executive Order 12127 merged multiple departments into the singular FEMA; these ranged from the National Weather Service Community Preparedness Program to the Federal Insurance Administration. FEMA also assumed responsibility for coordinating with state and local disaster response efforts. La Guardia might have noted that a majority of FEMA's tasks were "sissy." That focus was about to shift again.

President Reagan aimed his civil defense efforts on a space-based missile defense system known as "Star Wars"; his aggressive stance was another departure from the softer Eleanor Roosevelt–style efforts then being promoted by FEMA. And then the Berlin Wall fell in 1989, we "won" the Cold War, and peace was supposed to reign forever. Instead of contemplating the viability of Star Wars–style defense systems, President George H. W. Bush confronted a variety of environmental disasters during his tenure. He unexpectedly oversaw the *Exxon Valdez* oil-tanker spill in Alaska, Hurricane Hugo in Puerto Rico, Hurricane Andrew in south Florida, and the Loma Prieta earthquake in California.

Since these disasters knew no geographic limits, and the responses were often disorganized because of the events' duration and expansiveness, Bush's team promoted a national response effort that could be utilized across jurisdictions. Bush essentially supplemented Nixon's dual use mandate regarding equipment by promoting an all-hazards approach to planning. All-hazards unified the war-footing mentality of civil defense efforts with the more civilian-focused efforts of disaster-management response. This standard would come to be known as the Incident Command System (ICS)—essentially, an operational template to guide conduct in an emergency, regardless of the emergency's cause, size, location, or duration. ICS is a universal template, understood by all who may be called to a disaster. All first responders are trained in it; it sets a baseline and expectations for preparedness and response. It is led by a designated incident commander whose staff includes officers in public information, safety, operations, planning, logistics, and finance. In an ideal response scenario, these different commands work together to manage the destruction in an organized fashion. The beauty, if it can be called that, of the ICS is that it is exceptionally flexible, despite all its jargon; everyone from any emergency-response discipline knows how to plug into and play within the framework. So as a disaster gets bigger—say a wildfire crosses a state border, or demands more resources—the ICS expands in kind.

Dual-use, FEMA, and then ICS represented the growing sophistication of the nation's attitude toward emergency management. President Clinton continued that trend; he famously declared the head of FEMA part of the president's cabinet and placed a true expert, Arkansas's former head of emergency management and national disaster response leader James Lee Witt, in the post. As always, the range and nature of threats to the nation was shifting—or, better put, growing. In 1995, Timothy McVeigh and Terry Nichols killed 168 people at the Murrah building in Oklahoma City, just a month after the Aum Shinrikyo cult released nerve gas on three subway lines in Japan. In 1998, Osama bin Laden targeted the US embassies in Africa. A few days before Clinton left office, the USS *Cole* was attacked by Al Qaeda in the port of Aden, in Yemen.

But when President George W. Bush took over, his focus was elsewhere. Despite a growing chorus—including our report on the National Commission on Terrorism—of experts inside and outside government warning of the danger posed by bin Laden and the new terrorist threat, the first meeting of a new homeland security initiative occurred only a week before September 11, 2001.

There is a belief in expert circles that "9/11 changed everything." It is a truism so obvious, in many regards, that it is not worth challenging. But change also meant a form of amnesia. We forgot a lot of what the nation had already learned. We forgot that dual-use was the most effective and efficient way to protect our communities. We forgot that all-hazards training was the best means to support planning for first responders. We forgot that La Guardia made peace with Eleanor Roosevelt.

Though not always seamlessly, over the decades from Truman on, the two camps of preparedness had essentially merged. Our security needed the bunkers and sirens and militias as much as the community engagement, the volunteer responders, and citizen education.

Before 9/11, though, none of this history was of much consequence. At the Kennedy School, I certainly enjoyed academic debates with my colleagues, but I had to admit the conversation seemed a little precious. The outside world wasn't paying much attention to these issues; we were just a small academic program, barely thriving. I struggled to find funding for my researchers. We were set apart in an office away from the main campus and worked alone. It did feel a little lonely to me at the time. I grew more and more confident that working in counterterrorism and homeland security would not be a viable long-term professional plan. But at least I recognized how it allowed me to stay engaged with issues that I cared about. Plus, it was hard to argue with the position's flexible schedule.

And David and I soon learned that some flexibility would be needed. I was pregnant; our first baby was due in July 2001. We had been trying—I was now over thirty, after all—but it came as a surprise. I still felt too young. I was, despite running a domestic preparedness program, wholly unprepared for this stage of my life. I worried about the silliest things, including how the dog, Scout, would be able to cope. Sure, I was dealing with scary issues at work, but a baby? I had no idea what lay ahead, but I knew I would have to draw on all my resources: I would—in the lingo of my profession—be prepared, ready to confront this new normal. I would be ready for all hazards, dual-use my capabilities, invoke La Guardia when demands required, embrace Eleanor when parental instincts emerged.

I had a plan. And then, I didn't.

SEPTEMBER 11, 2001

CECILIA, OUR FIRST CHILD, WAS DUE ON JULY 21, 2001. WE COUNTED DOWN TO the date, sensing that we were crossing a bridge to our future. A bedroom in our townhouse was ready with new gear, stuff that we would soon realize was overpriced and underused—my compliments to the saleswoman who convinced me that I needed a pram. It didn't help that I bought two of everything, forgetting that there was a twenty-four-hour CVS pharmacy two blocks from our house. My mother had arrived from Los Angeles, and I was on leave from work. July 21 came and went. As did the 22nd, 23rd, 24th, and, dammit, the rest of the month. Adding to my discomfort, fatigue, and moodiness, the image of a happy home awaiting the arrival of a newborn was further shattered by my mother's growing impatience as she got progressively more anxious for the arrival of her seventh grandchild and the first child for her youngest daughter. I think, in the way only a mother can, she started to blame me.

We saw movies, like *A Beautiful Mind*, the professionally appropriate *Pearl Harbor*, *Shrek*, and *Legally Blonde*. We saw more movies. We saw double features. I even saw subtitled French films whose names I can't remember. I was desperate. I begged to be induced, but my doctor said that this delay was typical for the birth of a first child. I had gained over forty pounds and was well past the point of enjoying my pregnancy; I was fat, bloated, and prone to the equivalent of hot flashes, soaking my clothes in sweat. I started to drink a glass of wine at night, figuring anything that might get this baby out of my body was well justified.

On the afternoon of August 2, I finally, finally went into labor. We left for the hospital, but our well-practiced plans to get there quickly were foiled by the Red Sox, who began their game at Fenway while we were on our way to the Brigham and Women's Hospital. As we arrived at the parking lot, all I could think was that, at last, I would be a mom. The Red Sox lost to the Angels, 13-4. It might have been a sign of the night ahead for me.

Twenty-one hours of labor, and this child—a curse before a blessing—just wouldn't come out. The hospital seemed nonplussed by it all until both Cecilia and I showed signs of heart stress. Within seconds, from out of nowhere, doctors and nurses surrounded my bed and whisked me to an operating room, and after just a few minutes, Cecilia was born via an emergency C-section. It happened so fast, the response protocols of the hospital finely tuned and working in sync at the first signs of danger. David nearly missed the entire drama because he and my father took a short coffee break downstairs.

And there she was. About as perfect as any child could be, big and blond. David and I drove her home a few days later going about five miles an hour. We passed familiar places—where we first met, the site of our first date, our college dorms—then went up Massachusetts Avenue past my favorite pizza place and the gym where I planned on spending many hours that summer and fall. I was on maternity leave through January.

That August was not blissful. Let me be the first to say that I would have had a dozen children if they all arrived at six months old. The house, which we had set up in so carefully for our little one, quickly became a mess. I failed to follow the rule—sleep when your baby sleeps, however briefly—and became obsessed with writing thank-you letters and making sure Scout, who had until then been our only responsibility, didn't feel neglected. The news from the West Coast wasn't good, either; my father's mother, who had suffered from a decades-long illness, passed away within twenty-four hours of Cecilia's birth. The juxtaposition of life and death couldn't have been more pronounced. My parents left town, David went back to work, and I just didn't sleep. I never slept.

Neither did Cecilia, or at least not for long. Days and nights merged. David and I found ourselves eating salami sandwiches over the kitchen sink almost every evening. We were not exactly functioning adults those first few weeks.

I had imagined my daughter's arrival so differently—more like a Pampers ad where the showered new mother and well-tailored new father look at their precious baby in her crib, knowing she will sleep through the night and wake up with a dry diaper the next morning. I found showers optional for most of that month.

A friend of mine suggested that I take Cecilia to visit my sister in New York City. It would get me out of the house, at least. I was also looking forward to the opportunity to reassert my independence. I had always been an on-the-move professional woman. As a civil rights attorney and then, later, as a commissioner and fellow who traveled the globe, I never thought much of being on the go. I had always considered myself an excellent traveler—I don't suffer jet lag, I pack exceptionally light. I thought a trip to New York with Cecilia would remind me how much I loved being out and about in the world.

My parents agreed, and since their initial visit back east had been interrupted by my grandmother's funeral, we all decided to meet in the city on September 11, 2001.

That morning, I was ready. I had decided to take the train, as any flight seemed overwhelming at the time; trips from Logan Airport to La Guardia (the irony) were cheap, but though there was minimal security, with a newborn in tow, being close to the ground seemed more practical. I packed an arsenal of supplies, what must have been weeks' worth of onesies and bottles, toys and blankets, plus large gizmos like my breast pump and a forty-pound "newborn" stroller that was supposed to be easily deployed and refolded with one hand but which I hadn't quite mastered yet. I was ready for the wilderness of Manhattan, forgetting that the city has its fair share of babyGaps should I become desperate.

David drove me to the Amtrak train at South Station with the radio news turned up, like always. The host of the NPR program sounded short of breath.

While the broadcast was vague at first, it soon became clear that something had happened in downtown Manhattan. Some kind of aircraft had crashed into the north tower of the World Trade Center just a few minutes before. Emergency crews were on hand as people evacuated from the site. The mayor was en route to the scene.

As was I.

David and I discussed the news, but without images, we simply proceeded as planned. David was, I suspect, secretly grateful for the upcoming respite at home, as he was full-fledged into his second year of teaching, with tenure evaluations looming at every turn. He needed time to write and research, even if only for a few days.

The train did not change its schedule. I loaded my gear and placed Cecilia in her baby seat next to me. My cell phone rang. It was David calling, to let me know that the second tower had been hit.

Looking back, I wish I could explain my conduct. I wish my professional expertise had woken me up from the post-labor sleep deprivation that had taken hold of me. I wish the fact that I stubbornly kept to the plan, refused to pivot and respond—to practice the habits of grip—wasn't so inconsistent with what I knew to be true: planes don't simply crash into the World Trade Center accidentally.

I stayed on the train.

Disaster management studies always speak of our inability to recognize immediately that we are in harm's way; after plane accidents, flight attendants are trained to yell in passenger's faces that they have been in an accident and need to evacuate. And so there I was, heading straight for New York. It was as though I were a lifeguard swimming against the riptide; everything I knew as a professional did not make me alter my personal behavior. I told David I would arrive in the city in a few hours and then we would check in. The Amtrak train, following procedures that had never accounted for a terrorist attack—assuming the conductor had even known this was one—left the train station.

This was a time before iPhones. There was no Twitter, with its hasty and often erroneous firsthand accounts. No live streaming. There was simply no access to news. A man who had ventured to the train's café car in the hopes of finding a television told us that the only images on the screen were from a prerecorded National Geographic show on gorillas (the ape kind) in Rwanda.

The first phone call was from my good friend in the city who'd suggested the trip. She did not know I was taking the train and had just heard that the doomed flights had left from Logan en route to New York. It was just one of thousands of inaccuracies repeated that day—both flights had actually been bound for Los Angeles. I explained that I was still coming, and the thought never crossed her mind that I wouldn't. "I'll see you this afternoon," she responded. "I can't wait to meet Cecilia."

My mother was staying on the Upper West Side: safe, but able to see smoke and hear the sounds of tragedy. Her call began with a clear connection, but soon after, the line dropped. Cellular service capacity was overburdened that day. I called back. My mother explained that my father had already rented a car in Connecticut and they would make their way by cab to retrieve it and then, somehow, find me. She didn't want me coming into the city.

"Come on, Juliette," she begged. "You know exactly what this is."

My mother: in a few short words, she brought me back to reality. I did know exactly what this was, and I could no longer pretend that I didn't.

Although Cecilia stayed asleep, the passengers in my train compartment were hysterical—because of the events and also because of the wild rumors that were spreading everywhere. Accessing reliable information is essential in any crisis, and we were in a television-free train headed near Ground Zero with poor cell phone service. The reports coming in from family and friends who managed to call were incredible, but on that day, everything was possible to believe: President Bush had been killed, the Capitol had been hit by another plane, a dozen planes were down, the Twin Towers had fallen. The last was the only truth, and it was confirmed simply by consensus: This band of travelers had heard from too many different sources that the towers had, indeed, fallen.

Without images, it is hard to absorb exactly how skyscrapers fall. I assumed that they leaned and then crashed, destroying other buildings along the way, like a set of dominos along lower Manhattan. That they could both be destroyed like accordions seemed improbable—but, in hindsight, it was the best result, if "best" is really the right word.

I tried to call David but couldn't get through. As I hit Redial, my call waiting interrupted me. An unknown number came on the screen. It was NPR News. Then CNN. MSNBC. The BBC. The *Boston Globe*. The *New York Times*.

Us "terrorism experts" were an exceptionally small group. I had spoken in the media about Osama bin Laden before, and my status at Harvard, as well as my role on the commission, meant that many reporters—desperate to find anyone who knew anything—called my office, where my assistant gave them my cell phone number. My phone kept ringing, but I couldn't answer it. Cecilia was restless. I changed and nursed her, trying to ignore the noise around me. She quickly fell back asleep in her chair, and I grabbed some blank paper and a pen from my purse. I put my knees up to my chest, leaned against the train window, and returned the calls to do a series of interviews, some of them live. The questions were hardly profound. They showed just how rudimentary public knowledge about terrorism was at the time: who is this person, Osama bin Laden, and why do we keep hearing his name this morning; could anyone else have planned this; what happens now; where do we go from here?

I was the expert, giving history lessons about Afghanistan and Saudi Arabia and homeland security planning. I explained how the Taliban had offered a safe haven to bin Laden, as their agendas— destructive Islamic extremism—were similar. I reminded the reporters that Saudi Arabia had expelled bin Laden in the previous decade, despite his family's stature there, because they feared that his vision would turn against the undemocratic ruling royalty. I specifically noted that no federal agency was clearly in charge of the response. I spoke of New York's first responders' activities and the operational and technical challenges they were confronting, given the magnitude of the attack. The calls were coming in so frequently that I finished one radio interview while simultaneously nursing Cecilia for a second time. The producers didn't appear to hear what was happening on my end. It seemed perfectly normal to me that day, as if anything were normal that day, and my professional and personal lives merged on what was supposed to be a typical morning.

A young woman, weeping, heard me on the phone. She asked me who I was. "I work in this field," I answered, trying to be as generic as possible. She explained that she couldn't reach her family in the city where she lived. "I just want to go home," she said. "What should I do?"

I knew better than anyone: staying on that train was crazy, absurd, even dangerous. And I had done nothing to help those physically closest to me, nor the little one closest to my heart. The next stop was New Haven; we had stayed on that train for nearly 75 percent of the trip, and I was not going into the city with Cecilia. It was time I acted like the expert I was, and the mother I needed to be.

"We should all get off this train," I said rather loudly to no one in particular as I started to pull my bags and—damn this freaking thing!—open the forty-pound stroller.

The train was too noisy; my message wasn't getting through to anyone outside my aisle. So I stood up on a seat and gave my expert opinion, which was formed both in my head and my heart. I explained that we were risking our own safety by heading into New York, that there might be more attacks planned, and that at the very least we would find it a city we didn't want to be in. We should all get off the train, regardless of any plans we had and despite having no alternatives.

The other passengers all followed, because suddenly they had been given the green light to follow. They just needed the information, some direction for how they should behave and some guidance on how to protect themselves and others. And then my advice quickly got repeated, like a telephone operator game, through each train compartment.

Get off.

Get off.

Get off.

And they did.

The New Haven train station was crowded. Passengers were making their way down the platform, trying to get cell service to contact their families. Free water bottles were being distributed by train station employees. There was no pushing or shoving. As I carried my baby and gear across the platform, I didn't have to ask for help; strangers kept providing assistance because I was so loaded down. A Spanish-speaking waitress was pulled from a café to help some foreign visitors figure out their next moves. Though it was packed, the whole place was calm, determined, organized, and weirdly quiet. Everyone was holding their breath, it seemed.

I looked up and saw a group of people huddled intimately around a television set. These were the first images I could see of the attacks. Those images, replayed for days and years on end, never lose their power. And I understood, at last, the incomprehensible way that the towers fell.

I sat on the corner of the platform, holding my baby close to my chest. I was growing more and more agitated as I couldn't reach anyone, not even David.

A woman came up to me. "My son lives nearby," she said. "I saw that you got on in Boston. He's going to drive me back. We can give you a ride."

I thanked her, but declined. I had no car seat. The expert in me knew, despite everything happening that day, that the chances my baby would be harmed in a car accident were far greater than those of her being harmed in a terrorism incident. I didn't want to play any odds that day. I didn't want David to have to explain for the rest of his life, I thought, how we had died on 9/11 on the way back to Boston. "What were the chances?" I imagined him saying. Just the sound of his voice in my head made my arms shake, but I held firm and stayed put.

I knew two people in New Haven at the time. My good friend Emily Bazelon, the reporter and author, had just moved there from Cambridge. I kept trying her on my cell phone, but to no avail. For years afterward, she would remark that she still felt the guilt of not having been there to help, in a small way, that day. She was, as many mothers would be, out picking her sons up from school so she could have them close by. Adam Freed, a college friend, was spending a year at Yale after a successful stint as a television anchor. His later career—at Google and various Internet startups—would make him the monetary envy of many of our peers, but in 2001, he was a poor grad student living in a walk-up apartment. I finally got him on the phone.

"Adam," I said. "It's Juliette."

He didn't know I had just had my baby, and when I explained that we were at the train station, he barely needed to hear more. I did get into his car, justifying the risk by the minimizing impact of it being such a short trip. As soon as we arrived at his place, I ran to his landline. Cell service was still just intermittent.

I finally reached David on his landline at work; he had been trying to reach me, but couldn't get through. He sounded relieved and asked me where I was.

"I'm such an idiot for letting you get on that train. What was I thinking?" he said apologetically. "Did you know then?"

"Maybe I did; I just don't know. It's so obvious now, just a few hours later," I replied. I told him about the trip, and the media calls, and my advice to the other passengers. He said he had just heard that Amtrak was stopping all trains into the city and that the bridges were closing to traffic. My parents would spend the night in the city and make their way to Cambridge on Wednesday, the 12th.

"They don't have to do that," I told David.

"I think they know you're going back to work. I think," he said apologetically, "that you're going back to work."

As soon as I hung up, David jumped into our car and started driving toward New Haven. He had the car seat. We couldn't predict if traffic would be heavy or not, so we had no idea how long the trip would take. "I'll get there as fast as I can," he promised. "And I'll bring you home."

Adam and I spent a few hours in front of the television, switching between channels as if this would somehow change the news. Fortunately, I had packed everything and more, with spares and redundancies built in. It is an instinct that can make us safer at home and for the homeland: do not put all your eggs in one basket, because if something fails, you may need an alternative plan. That I was fully prepared also gave me some solace—Cecilia was comfortable, as was I. I had what I needed, and my baby was safe.

Adam played with Cecilia on his apartment floor, using pots and pans for makeshift drums. He sang and tried to get a smile out of her. He was winging it, and I was immensely grateful. It also gave me a little time to touch base with family and friends, or at least the ones I could contact. I needed those few moments to get my bearings. I answered some e-mails, wishing all to whom I wrote much love. I am not one for "xoxo"s, but on this day, the sentiment seemed appropriate. Many of the notes came from friends who had worried that I was on a plane. I wrote back that the Logan departures were bound for the West Coast: the terrorists had wanted them large and fully loaded with petroleum for massive explosions and maximum effect. God, I hated the details of my job.

When David finally arrived in New Haven, we held each other in the doorway of Adam's apartment. I know I wasn't suffering in the way so many victims and their families did that day, but I felt such a tremendous sense of loss. I wanted September 10, 2001. I wanted to be a tired new mother who didn't care about the news. I wanted to be professionally irrelevant. I wanted to be home. I had thought I would feel more relief at David's arrival, but then again, we still had a journey ahead. Cecilia was safe, and David was with me, but somehow I felt unmoored. Home. That would surely settle my soul.

We drove in near silence. I was done listening to the radio; I was experiencing an odd phenomenon wherein events simultaneously change quickly and don't change at all, and it became necessary to tune it all out. I turned my phone off, too; there would be plenty of time for interviews later. I was in the backseat with Cecilia, my hand to her heart. She knew nothing of the world around her, and I was both grateful and envious.

The lanes of the highway were clear and the drive took only just over two hours, a scarily fast pace. We were all in a hurry. American flags had already been tied to overpasses. Helicopters—large, military ones—flew overhead, searching for something, anything. State troopers lined certain tollbooths—all open and free of charge—but they were not focused on issuing traffic tickets. Like first responders across the country, they quickly adapted to a threat that they thought would never be theirs. A terrorist attack on American soil was not part of their basic training.

We lived on a dead-end street, in an area of Cambridge that was becoming somewhat gentrified. New town houses built by professional couples with young children stood next to triplex intergenerational family homes of lifelong Porter Square residents, people who remember that this was where the porterhouse steak was created and where Tip O'Neill got his start.

As we headed down the narrow road and turned onto Regent Street, we saw a crowd of parents and kids around a bunch of tables and chairs. We heard music coming from someone's stereo, aimed outdoors through the windows. Elderly Portuguese ladies had babies on their laps; an inflatable pool had been set up in the corner of someone's driveway; a few water balloons were being tossed. Lawyers and doctors who I never saw during the weekdays were in shorts and T-shirts. A barbecue grill was lit; there were trays of chips and salsa, watermelon slices, and cookies. Kids had regained a day of summer, and their parents and other grownups looked on, believing that a neighborhood party was a reclaiming of our innocence.

We parked our car and applause spontaneously erupted from our neighbors, most of whom did not know us personally. Of course, we said hello occasionally. Sometimes, we received a phone call letting us know that Scout had wandered into a neighbor's backyard. We were all friendly, but there were no deep affections among us.

"You made it, thank god," Alison, a stay-at-home mother of two, yelled. She looked truly giddy, elated. "We just thought we need to make this day about our kids, that we were all here. We saw David leave," she said to me as I got out of the car, "and heard you on the radio. David left the door unlocked so we could walk Scout. She's doing fine." I hugged her, because it just felt like the right thing to do.

"I had no idea that's what you did for a living!" Alison said to me. "There was no reason to until today. It's kind of relevant now." I remember her laughing at those last words. She continued, "I guess that's an understatement, right?"

I was too tired to stay outside long. David put Cecilia in her crib, greeted Scout, and then walked to the nearby mini-mart for bread, milk, and some deli sandwiches. It was growing darker outside, but nightfall would bring no solace. I talked to my parents, who were staying inside that night in New York. I caught up on the news, managed some of the media requests, and planned to visit a nearby television studio the next day to begin my new role as a "terrorism expert commentator." I hate to admit it, but I kept thinking about what I would wear: I was fat and tired, and I didn't even know what clothes in my closet still fit.

After bathing Cecilia and putting her down for what I hoped would be at least four hours, I took a final call from BBC Radio. I heard that very segment ten years later, played back to me by the same show as part of the tenth-anniversary coverage. I was in full expert mode in the segment, giving a take on the events based on professional experience only a few years long. I knew I had significantly more knowledge than most. I spoke like an objective bystander, despite what had happened on the train, calmly trying—how could I even try?—to put that day into context. I sounded authoritative, despite how I felt. Listening to myself so many years later, I was taken aback by my demeanor. It was as if the expert persona had rid me of all softness. I was all La Guardia, with no Eleanor.

On that day, I put the phone down and then, finally, at long last, I cried. I cried until my shoulders shook, until my throat burned, until I felt relief. It was an uncontrollable cry, a cry that would have been familiar in every home that day.

David looked over and came to my side. The tenuous nature of my own expertise that day was hidden from everyone but him. "Some expert analysis," he said, trying to get a smile out of me.

I'm no expert, I thought. I'm a mom.

The next decade would teach me that the two were not so incompatible after all.

THE SIREN CALL
OF HOME

IT IS DIFFICULT TO RELATE WHAT HAPPENED IN THOSE DAYS AND WEEKS immediately following the attacks. Something had changed, but it wasn't quite clear what. For me, those weeks were a blur of activity, new motherhood, and newfound purpose. My program at the Kennedy School was suddenly relevant, and so we ramped up on staff and funding. We were seen as prescient. My days of relative anonymity in the academic bureaucracy were over. I became—since I didn't actually have much real responsibility—a frequent commentator in news and print media, and traveled to DC for government briefings and testimony.

I went through the motions, but I was almost paralyzed, as so many of us were, by exhaustion, anger, and fear. And sadness. The American flags waving everywhere—I know they were intended to inspire, but every time I saw one, it just brought back images from that Tuesday.

And I was suffering. By nature, I am a relatively happy person, somewhat quirky and uninspired by existential angst. It isn't that I'm necessarily the life of the party, but despite my career, I tend to be relatively optimistic. I am smiling in every childhood picture taken of me. David has often remarked that I have only two bad moods: April 15 every year, when our taxes are due, and any morning before I have had my first cup of coffee.

Maybe it was postpartum depression; maybe it was 9/11-induced despair, compounded by my feelings as a new mom. How can I judge what were normal feelings? Since, by September 12, my anticipated maternity leave was long gone, the cause of my depression was irrelevant. I bought new black shirts and oversized blazers to fit over my nursing bras, and flowing skirts to hide my pregnancy weight. I didn't exercise, though I knew it would help.

David urged me to take some real time to recover.

"This can all wait. It's not going away," he told me after I'd recovered from another heavy and tearful mood swing. The classes could be delayed, the books written another time, the television segments rescheduled. "It's twenty-four-seven news," he reminded me. "It will be around later." He was right, but I would have none of it. I felt like I needed to keep busy, contribute in whatever way I could. Cecilia would be fine, I told myself, as I left her crying in her crib while I took a conference call that at the time seemed so pressing.

Publicly, I looked together. I graciously smiled at all who commented on my composure. The only benefit of my depression was my plummeting weight, which, as any new mother knows, isn't pure vanity. Getting back to where I had once been physically was a sign that I could recover. But mentally, I still felt isolated from friends, family, and, worst of all, Cecilia. The little things I needed to do to make our home function, like going to the market, became unbearable burdens. I ignored the techniques I had always used to "reboot," such as running or taking yoga classes. I was disorganized, completely forgetting my sister, Marisa's, birthday. I was short with my parents, getting annoyed at them for any reason I could find. I was not myself. Nothing was working.

I needed help. I wasn't sleeping. Like so many others, I couldn't snap back to normal. I simply couldn't separate the sadness I felt about the world from the stresses I felt as a new, working mother. I needed to talk to someone.

I finally visited a therapist in late September who prescribed medication for my postpartum depression. The drugs were remarkable; they helped me reclaim some sense of stability, even in a time of national angst. I was not alone; even my therapist jokingly noted that "9/11 was a growth industry." But I never admitted my feelings at the time. I was ashamed at what I incorrectly viewed as a sign of weakness. I never disclosed the fact that I'd taken the medications until years later, when I rejoined the federal government and had to admit it during yet another security clearance review.

At the time, I couldn't go back into government, mostly because—pretty early on—I strongly criticized some of the tactics of the Bush administration. In particular, the administration made it clear that it planned on invading Iraq, under the guise of fighting the war on terror. This seemed a fatal mistake, the most fatal of all. I had no premonition about the war in Iraq, but years of listening to my family had made me aware of the campaign's pros and cons. The next time we think about starting a war in an Arab country, I suggest its architects have dinner with the Deeb and Kayyem clans. Anyone from that part of the world knew that the notion of a peaceful occupation was delusional. "Have they met the Arabs?" my brother, Jon, who lived in California with his family, said to me over the phone of Vice President Cheney's early promises of peace breaking out all over. Of course, Jon was operating under the basic principle that any ethnic group may make broad generalizations about our own kind.

I used my perch to provide a counternarrative to what was too often defended as being necessary—whether it was Iraq, racial profiling, or the Guantánamo Bay detention camp. I would go on air or speak at a conference and often would find myself on the battering end of incredulous cross-examinations. It wasn't that I was a naysayer; my goodness, I had devoted a few years to homeland security efforts already. But the breathless moves we were making—a war with no strategy, a push for airline security efforts that targeted citizens who looked different, a foreign prison with no rights afforded those sent there—were mistakes we would be able to see clearly if we could just look past our anger. My skepticism even led to a dinner with the late, great Senator Ted Kennedy, at which we discussed his eventual vote against the war. Democrats going against the Republican administration, and most of our own party, were accused of something only slightly short of treason. The former military weapons expert and Iraq War advocate David Kay, who would later lead an independent search for weapons of mass destruction in Iraq, called me a "modern-day Neville Chamberlain" during a debate, pointedly linking Hitler to Hussein and Bush critics to Nazi sympathizers. Years later, when he famously came back from Iraq to admit that "we were all wrong," I felt like asking who exactly "we" was.

I felt like a goldfish in a pool of sharks. I flinched at the cockiness of so many who orchestrated the war on terror, a term I despised but would likewise come to use as shorthand. I felt that term was too brutal and broad; so dismissive of the challenges and dissent in any democracy. I suspect that was the point.

And not too long after 9/11, it got very personal.

On October 5, 2001, Robert Stevens, who worked at a tabloid called *The Sun*, died after entering a Florida hospital with an undiagnosed illness that caused vomiting and shortness of breath. Eventually, it became clear that someone was sending weaponized anthrax by mail to members of the media and political leaders. The first letter was sent just a week after 9/11, but the lethal consequence of the attack was only discovered in October. The question was obvious, as was the answer for so many: Was Al Qaeda launching its next wave—an invisible wave—of terrorism?

The threat of biological terror—invisible, odorless, passed from friend to friend, child to child—raises distinct fears in our interconnected society. The anthrax letters that were sent to media personalities and political leaders would send the federal government on a multiyear chase, focusing on one possible culprit (Al Qaeda), then another (Steven Hatfill), then, finally, another (Bruce Ivins). Ivins was a scientist at the government's biodefense labs at Fort Detrick in

Frederick, Maryland. On July 27, 2008, as federal authorities began to make a case against Ivins nearly seven years after it all began, he took an overdose of acetaminophen and died.

But in 2001 we knew none of this. What Americans knew at the time was that we were vulnerable. And uninformed. And not well positioned to address this kind of attack. The Bush administration, still forming tactics to fight international terror, was flat-footed in its response and in its advice to the public.

For several months in 2001 and 2002, the anthrax attack and the hoaxes that followed put tremendous stress on the public safety and public health communities, which were forced to isolate and test potential victims. Tom Ridge, the former governor of Pennsylvania, resigned his executive office four days after 9/11 to become President Bush's point person on homeland security—there was as yet no department to speak of. Ridge and former Wisconsin governor and secretary of health and human services Tommy Thompson led the federal government's response to the anthrax attacks. They consistently bumped up against each other, sometimes publicly. Thompson would lose much credibility when he announced that one of the victims came in contact with anthrax from water in a creek, thereby terrifying everyone who drank water or lived near a creek. He had no scientific or medical background. The anthrax letters were horribly dangerous, killing five people and infecting seventeen. One victim, Stevens, received a letter. Two others died from exposure whose source is still undetermined: one was a Vietnamese immigrant in the Bronx and the other a ninety-four-year old widow from Connecticut. The last two were employees of the infamous Brentwood post office facility in Washington, DC, through which anthrax letters addressed to senators passed. While Senate staffers and *New York Times* reporters were carefully treated for potential exposure, mail workers at the Brentwood facility were essentially told to go back to work. The deaths there, where employees were mostly African-American and without much protection, exposed some of the racial and class divisions often encountered during any disaster response. After an uproar, Brentwood was closed, and would not reopen for another twenty-six months as the site was decontaminated.

The country was unnerved, again, suspecting Al Qaeda. I didn't think that that was the case. Whatever the reason for the anthrax attacks, there was no evidence to conclude Al Qaeda had launched them. And explaining to the nation why this was so, surely, was where a security expert in a university-funded program on domestic preparedness could make a difference. I marshaled my thinking.

For one, as was proved clearly by 9/11, Al Qaeda wanted to kill lots of people in a spectacular way. Anthrax was a silent death that couldn't produce the dramatic visuals that generated press coverage and triggered mass shock. It had taken several weeks just to identify the cause of Stevens's death. Yes, the fear of anthrax resulted in tremendous speculation and mounting chaos as the government failed to deliver accurate and scientifically sound information, but it didn't have that "watch this" feel to which I knew Al Qaeda aspired. In December 2001, for instance, an Al Qaeda affiliate, Richard Reid, tried to detonate explosives on a commercial jetliner: That was what Al Qaeda coveted, and if Reid had been successful, it would have been a huge victory for them.

Second, bin Laden was not taking credit for the anthrax attacks, even as he continued to release videos and statements one after the other. In those days, he was exceptionally popular in certain parts of the world, and the opportunity to boast of bringing the United States to its knees again would have been too good to pass up. It was clear there were other attacks planned—much of the Middle East and parts of Europe would also feel his wrath—but anthrax didn't fit into the model of his form of radical terrorism. And he was conspicuously silent on the subject.

But, most important, my prior work in the field had taught me that the use of anthrax and other weaponized high-grade biological agents was a coveted technique among white supremacists and home-grown reactionaries long before 9/11. This was in my wheelhouse. I had read papers, sat through briefings, and been privy to classified evidence, which led to a conclusion: The choice of weapon was consistent with a long line of failed attempts by American terrorists who were (often) Christian, former military, and passionate haters of government and the mainstream media.

It did not seem exceptionally controversial to say so on television. On the contrary, it seemed precisely the sort of thing a security expert ought to say, drawing on her expertise to offer an alternative to the frenzied public reaction to the fact that deadly anthrax was showing up in some people's mailboxes. Americans might actually find it empowering to know that Al Qaeda wasn't behind every bad thing that happened. Maybe I should not have said "former military"—it wasn't, in the end, accurate—but the radicalization of former military had been a concern of the National Commission on Terrorism. Maybe my delivery could have been more polished, though I doubt either of these things would have mattered much. Maybe I could have chosen a different network.

Fox News was the Bush network, supporting the war agenda by focusing its analysis and experts on presenting a narrative that led in only one direction: war. Some analysts work directly for networks; it was a role I would later fill first for NBC News and then, after my government stints, for CNN. Until I was offered one, I did not know that although these exclusive contracts have monetary benefits, often they pay you simply so you don't appear on a competing channel. At this time, I was a free agent and went on Fox because they asked. In a studio in the suburbs of Boston, I sat alone in a room with a camera and a backdrop. I could see what viewers were seeing live from a small television on the floor, directly under the camera. And that was how I could tell that the Fox News anchor didn't seem too happy with my answer. He lurched forward, maybe hoping to wring my neck from afar, and waved his index finger at me.

"What?! Do you think this is just a coinkydink?" he asked.

I had never heard the term "coinkydink" before. I had no idea whether I should answer yes or no. Who says "coinkydink" on television? So I just repeated my analysis, which I hoped was the point of having me interviewed by a news anchor in the first place: to put forward a piece of evidence that could be weighed by a public ready to blame Al Qaeda for everything that could go wrong.

And, yes, it was a coinkydink.

Which hardly mattered. What did matter was the fact that my statements didn't fit into a narrative then being formed that blamed all horrors on foreign terrorists. My words, which some deemed the equivalent of heresy, were also repeated on national right-wing radio stations. The hate commentary was predictable: How dare I accuse an American of such madness? Was I an Al Qaeda sympathizer? This was, they argued, the kind of thinking that made us vulnerable and unwilling to take the aggressive steps necessary to protect ourselves and our country.

I had no idea any of this was going on until I walked into my office at the Kennedy School the next morning to more than four hundred e-mails from people with addresses like "donttreadonme," "secondamendment," and "skinnylegs." I don't know why this last one stood out; it may have been because I was coveting them. All four hundred e-mails were unkind. Some were cruel, some threatening. I was not only an Al Qaeda sympathizer, but also a hater of white men—David, as a Jew, did not seem to qualify. Oh yes, the few who had done their research knew that part of my bio as well.

Many of them were exceptionally racist and xenophobic, equating my lineage with anti-American sentiments and pro-terrorist tendencies. "What's the two 'y's about in your last name?" one e-mailer wondered. "No Americans have two 'y's." I didn't reply, but when I spoke to my brother, Jon, he did have a nice retort that he called the "Manchurian wife conspiracy theory."

"Think about it," he said to me one night on the phone. "Here you are, an Arab-American with family in the Middle East, top schools, government service, married to a nice Jewish professor, and with top security clearance. They must be freaking out. You've, like, infiltrated the whole thing, like the Manchurian candidate." This from the guy who was on the Unabomber's short list.

I knew enough to read and save all the e-mails, however painful. I created a new e-mail folder, entitled it "Crazies," and filed all of them away. I sent to the school's security department one that was particularly violent, mostly just to keep a record should he come back to haunt me. Indeed, if you ever find yourself at the receiving end of a flurry of hate, save all the e-mails or tweets or Facebook posts. I have learned over the years that most e-mail haters tend to annoy only once, fortunately; one and done. But keep track, just in case. If a threat is violent and specific in nature, notify the authorities. If the hater tries to contact you three times or more, notify the authorities. Do not reply. Do not defend. Do not engage.

After a day, they all seemed to go away. Life, as they say, went on. The confused response to the anthrax attack continued, starkly revealing the limitations of our nascent homeland security efforts. I returned to my day job, which wasn't much solace given the nature of my day job.

So I all too casually opened up an anonymous letter that came to my office a few days later. My address was in a handwritten scrawl, but I didn't pay much attention. And then I noticed white powder on my desk. Not a lot of white powder, but enough to completely freak me out. The letter said something like, "Have fun."

The expert in me knew the drill. Do not leave the office. It's irresponsible. It could expose others. Do not go near children, or anyone else for that matter. Immediately contact the police. It is your responsibility to the rest of society to behave like a rational human being and think through the consequences of what you are doing.

I knew that. I got through some of the checklist: I picked up the phone, called the police, explained what had happened, and called my assistant on the other side of the door so she could inform my colleagues and the mailroom staff. I tried to calm my nerves. I moved away from my desk. So far, so good.

But wait.

I then opened my office door and walked out. This wasn't part of the drill. I left to go home to be with Cecilia before any authorities came to check on the powder. I believed I was the victim of a hoax mailing, just as hundreds of others had been. I couldn't prove it, obviously, but exposure wasn't my concern. I admit this simply because my real fear had nothing to do with me: My god, I thought, if they found me at work, then they could surely find me at home, where Cecilia was taking a nap.

There is no question it was a stressful time, no doubt I was suffering from postpartum depression, no debate that the government's response was abysmal and did not inspire confidence. But I was going on pure instinct. And sometimes, instinct is bad.

If people went after me by e-mail, or if someone sent a letter to my work, how far of a leap would it be for them to find my home, where Cecilia was? It didn't seem that far-fetched a notion. But leaving that office was a mistake.

If I had followed the protocols that were written by experts like me, I would have stayed put, isolated myself, and waited to be tested while receiving a dose of antibiotics. Instead, I walked the mile to our house, surprised the nanny, and held Cecilia as I fielded calls from the university police. The Cambridge police had sent the biohazmat team into my office, where they found the letter next to my half-drunk coffee. That team notified the state authorities; they had no choice but to take this incident seriously. I gave them the context of the last few days and the e-mails that had come in. They asked for my e-mail password and started culling the saved threats.

They did not seem annoyed at my behavior, and I was grateful for that. Lord knows I had given them cause. After all, the target of the letter, Harvard's in-house terror expert, might have just exposed everyone between her office and her house, including her baby. They sent a team to my home as well to check our mail and, I suspect, ensure I stayed put.

A colleague, who was kind enough not to judge me, called to explain what was unfolding at my office. Firemen had arrived in full biological decontamination gear, oversized men in oversized protective suits with those huge masks over their heads. Protocols were barely in place, so there was no immediate e-mail notification to those who were nearby. The students filing out of the building, the faculty and staff spying those alien-looking firemen, all must have been wondering if they were breathing a highly lethal substance.

The substance in question did not have the granularity of weaponized anthrax; it was too large and flaky. It was powdered sugar. And as with so many hoaxes, there were insufficient resources to find out who had sent it. The authorities seemed certain that the jokester was not tied directly to anyone who had sent me one of those e-mails. I wasn't then and am not now so sure.

A coinkydink if I ever saw one.

I am well aware that mine was hardly model behavior: I had placed my family and colleagues in danger because of my overwhelming desire to be home. Writing it now, it seems so insane that all I can do is offer it up as a best lesson from the worst action.

And the lesson is rather simple: The desire to be home, to protect those in our home, is a force not to be trifled with. It was the same feeling I had on 9/11, that sense that I just needed to be back in my familiar surroundings. It is like tunnel vision, and I convinced myself that there was simply no way I had been exposed. I am well aware that if I was wrong in my prediction, Cecilia would not have survived.

I can't take it all back. But I believe I can use my own experience to empower those who would be similarly focused on their home. I get it. Home is like a safe base in Tag. That's where you want to be. But that instinct isn't always right. It is the same irrational desire that makes otherwise sane people refuse to listen to evacuation orders.

If home is where, physically, you and your family will be safest, then by all means get there or stay there if you can. But if that journey (or staying put) could expose you or your family to some grievous harm, then forget your instincts. You are your own worst enemy at this stage. Go with your brain, and not your gut. I learned this the hard way.

And I can say this now only because the envelope tested negative for anthrax. I try not to think about the consequences if the test had come out the other way.

IDEOLOGY IS FOR LOSERS

FOR THE FOLLOWING YEAR OR SO, MY POSITION AT THE KENNEDY SCHOOL allowed me some degree of flexibility. I knew I was lucky: I could remain engaged with the issues of our time but also manage my responsibilities at home. And those responsibilities, in May 2003, grew to include Leo, our first son.

My predilection to reduce risk led me to choose to give birth, again, via C-section rather than try to deliver vaginally. It was then I learned that government agencies are not the only entities to utilize acronyms with abandon; I read extensively about the VBAC (vaginal birth after C-section) debates, but chose the road that felt safer to me. Since Leo came into the world weighing more than ten pounds, I feel I made the right decision. In the operating room, our petite doctor called for assistance; Leo was so big she couldn't lift him.

Unlike Cecilia, who was an easy baby born in uneasy times, Leo was born during a more stable period in our lives. David had tenure, I was comfortable in my career, and though the times—while we were at war in Afghanistan and then Iraq—were tense, they weren't characterized by the chaos of 9/11.

But we soon discovered that taking care of Leo would come with its own challenges. He was—and I love you, Leo—a difficult, unbearable, frightening, inconsolable baby. He never fit into newborn clothes and went straight to nine-to-twelve-month onesies. He was uncomfortable all the time and rarely slept. He cried incessantly. All the luxuries that our lives afforded us—money, air-conditioning in the hot summer months, a network of people ready to help—couldn't put him at ease. Cecilia, now in pigtails, thought her little brother was hilarious. She would pat his belly to quiet him—which rarely worked. Every night that summer, I would walk Leo up and down Massachusetts Avenue as he wailed and cried. I started to look so disheveled that a kind shop vendor once asked me, when he saw me on yet another late-night walk with a crying Leo, if I needed a shelter to stay in.

I often worried something was wrong with him. "He's a baby," David reminded me. "They cry. He just cries a little more." At his six-week appointment, I joked with our doctor about whether I couldn't get a refund. He suggested that maybe Leo—whom we started calling "the linebacker" for his expansive physique—wasn't getting enough food from me. I had nursed Cecilia successfully for almost a year, slowly transitioning to formula, then baby food, then the real thing. Six weeks old seemed too early to introduce a bottle.

It was not my fault, our doctor told us, but as with many things in life, the capacity and the need didn't match. So I reluctantly put together a first bottle, and Leo's hand jolted out of his blanket as he held it to his mouth. He drank all eight ounces—for any parents out there, this is some record, I know. And with that, my adaptive skills came into play. I would just have to practice the habits of grip—to amend the plan. Leo needed something different, and I wasn't going to complain as he peacefully slept, his cheeks red, his knees under his chest, his butt up in the air. I believe he quickly moved to steaks. He was happy and content, and so were we.

But I still worried that somehow I had failed the maternal gods. I called my sister, whose urban wisdom—doled out in texts and quick phone calls—has guided me much of my life. "You're going to feel guilty because you can't breast-feed? My god, get over it. Don't you get plenty of zealots at work? Move on," Marisa said. "Ideology is for losers."

She was right. But I felt like I was encountering backward ideology everywhere, as a mother and as an expert. As David and I managed two children under two, with careers, I was never inclined to answer the question, "How are you managing?" I'm just not interested in the work-life balance discussions, the infamous mommy wars, the never-ending debates that result in a draw. My experience is simply that, if we are lucky, our lives are long and move in ways that are often unpredictable. Most of my friends are the same in this regard.

I was firmly in an ebb stage of my ebb-and-flow career. I felt pangs of jealousy as I read about the accomplishments and career advancement of colleagues and peers. On most days, when the kids were young, my reigning philosophy was akin to "duck and cover" until the kids were asleep, the dishwasher was loaded, and I could get a few hours of sleep to prepare for another day of weaving, bobbing, and dealing.

I'm not into grand theories. And if I found parental dogmatism unbecoming and unhelpful at home, in the office I was losing tolerance for the ideological certitude that animated so many of the national security discussions of those times. Even the words we used to describe America's security challenges at that time illustrated how spectacularly our imaginations had failed us. We imagined that we were a nation whose strength was solely defined by our invincibility. How we discussed 9/11, how we waged a "war on terror," reflected how grossly we misunderstood homeland security. Especially those two words first uttered by President George W. Bush and repeated often to defend policies as far-ranging as the war in Iraq and the Patriot Act: "Never again."

"Never Again." That idea is as absurd as it is simplistic. It is as vague as it is damaging. No two words have ever provided so little meaning or context; no catchphrase has ever so warped policy discussions that it has permanently confused the public's understanding of homeland security. It convinced us that invulnerability was a possibility. Remember: sh-t happens.

It was a fantasy. And we knew it then. Indeed, as early as October 2001, as anthrax letters arrived in mailboxes in Florida, Washington, and New York, even President Bush admitted the idea of America's invulnerability was an unhelpful way to think about homeland security. It was then that he told his new homeland security advisor, former governor Tom Ridge, that the country's tightened controls at our borders with Canada and Mexico had created too much backlog. This, in turn, had undermined the economic engine that sustains relations with our largest trading partners. The leaders of both nations had already called Bush, who in turn told Ridge, as he later described in his memoir, to find a "better way." Something had to give. The president and author of "Never Again" told his newly appointed security czar that for America to be America, we had to accept a certain amount of vulnerability. This was only a month after 9/11.

Still, I watched as "Never Again" was used to initiate the war in Iraq. "Never Again" also gave justification for any government investment that would advance the so-called war on terror in the homeland. Money kept flowing: a landlocked jurisdiction bought a boat; homeland security money purchased air-conditioning for trash trucks. My Kennedy School program, even, found itself swimming in new funds from public and private grants.

The normal public policy discussions that usually occur about investments—does the program work? Is it necessary? Are there cheaper alternatives?—did not take place when we promised each other "Never Again." It was so easy to invest more, do more, spend more, simply because the alternative—that something bad could happen—was not acceptable.

Among all its flaws, the worst aspect of "Never Again" was that it let the experts run the show. Average Americans delegated responsibility for their security. To prove the idiocy of such a notion, all any of us really needed to do was quickly review an ordinary week: There are always ups and downs. "Never Again" just doesn't exist in our day-to-day world, in which mundane bad things—cars breaking down, kids or parents getting inconveniently sick, jobs turning stressful—actually happen all the time. Of course, after 9/11 we were so angry, so convinced of our greatness, that no countervailing theory really stood a chance against "Never Again." We all wanted to believe what the experts promised.

This kind of thinking made any effort to involve Americans in taking safety measures look comical. When the Bush administration did try to engage its citizens—as with Tom Ridge's infamous request for Americans to buy duct tape in the event of a biological or chemical attack, or the much-discussed color-code system—the efforts seemed amateur. They were easily mocked.

I knew that invulnerability was total baloney. You didn't have to be a security expert to see the holes in their argument. Parents who do everything they can to protect a child from scrapes and bruises will find themselves in a pharmacy's first-aid section just like the rest of us. We can minimize risks, but we should never say "Never Again."

But a false ideology isn't improved on by claiming a different one. Yet in 2005, as the war in Iraq proved less easy than promised, a motto emerged that would move some in post-9/11 America in a wildly different direction. Get your yoga mats, sunglasses, and margaritas, people. This is how we roll: "Keep Calm and Carry On."

This ubiquitous mantra is presumed to represent the British World War II mentality of stiff upper lips, and stands in stark contrast to our efforts in the very different global war on terror. The terrorist attacks of 9/11 had unleashed a response that was grand, noisy, violent, and anything but calm. "Keep Calm and Carry On" gained traction quickly in the United States as our wars proved unable to keep us safe and secure. Its ever-increasing popularity was partially measured by where it started to appear—everywhere from cooking aprons to a popular iPhone case—and its witty pop-culture variants like "Keep Calm and Drink More Water," "Keep Calm and Bite Me," and "Keep Calm and Call Me, Maybe." If only Americans could master a Zen-like calmness, we could, like those World War II Britons, bravely face an uncertain future. We just needed to take a chill pill.

Not to be disrespectful to our friends across the pond, but that phrase, evoking images of stiff upper lips as Hitler conquered most of Europe and terrorized London with his aerial bombardments, is a total (in British English) fib. It gives the false sense that the best way to approach looming disaster is simply to keep doing what you're doing. If "Never Again" risked convincing the nation that invulnerability was an achievable goal, "Keep Calm" risked convincing the nation that we should simply stop trying to reduce those vulnerabilities. Every aspect of the approach is wrong, including its history.

Over a million copies of a poster bearing the words "Keep Calm and Carry On" were printed in the United Kingdom on the eve of World War II, as men dutifully prepared to fight, children went to the countryside, and women left their homes to work in offices and factories. The phrase itself was commissioned in 1939 by the British government, along with the less-than-pithy "Freedom Is in Peril" and "Your Courage, Your Cheerfulness, Your Resolution Will Bring Us Victory."

Britain's whole "Keep Calm" thing is a fiction, though. It never happened. No one knows specifically why the "Keep Calm" public education campaign was dropped during World War II, but it never saw the light of day. It wasn't until 2000 that Stuart Manley, a bookseller from Northumberland, England, found the poster from World War II while rummaging through several boxes of books he had bought at an auction. He put a copy of it on the wall in his store, Barter Books, in Alnwick. Some customers asked about it; others begged for copies. Then a national newspaper reported on Manley's find. After that, in an ironic description given the tone of the poster's message, Manley said, "All hell broke loose." "Keep Calm" spread like wildfire around the globe.

I have a theory as to why those posters moldered for decades: Churchill knew that ideology is for losers. Those charged with ensuring Britain's survival under the threat of invasion knew that "Keep Calm and Carry On" was not the motto its subjects needed. Resiliency isn't calm. Preparedness isn't calm. Churchill needed Londoners to engage and sacrifice to keep the engines of commerce moving in the nation's capital, even as bombs fell on the city. Their strength wasn't the result of a public relations campaign; it was a war effort, as carefully constructed as any battle. It was grip.

True grip does not reside in some motto; it cannot be fully delegated to some government agency; it isn't about a state of mental Zen. Unless we understand this basic fact, we will believe that who lives and who dies during a crisis, who rebounds from disaster and who succumbs to it, simply reflects the luck of the draw. There is a certain amount of fate involved, but wishful thinking isn't very sound strategy, at least not for a citizen. Or a parent.

These ideological extremes, however, were all the public had to guide their thinking about the homeland's security in the years after 9/11. And they both failed us. I recognized at the time that the power of my perch was limited, but thought that through books and teaching and public policy debates, I could move the needle just a little. I could remind the public what they know from living their lives every day: sh-t happens. And a citizenry that accepted those two words as a basic fact could call for security efforts that would make us, and our families, more resilient should danger come to pass.

Never Again: It's bull.

Keep Calm and Carry On: It's a myth.

Sh-t Happens: Now you got this.

True, I wasn't an advisor to a governor or an assistant secretary, nor did I hold a title that gave me exceptional authority. But I soon figured out that those weren't the only roles that could provide me with an opportunity to make my case. After all, I did have one lofty position: I was on the board of directors of my growing brood's day care center.

THE DAY CARE DIARIES

IN EARLY 2005, I LEARNED I WAS PREGNANT AGAIN. IT WASN'T A SURPRISE; David and I both came from families with three children, so, over the course of five years, we simply repeated the legacy we had inherited.

Let me state the obvious: by the third child, there is really nothing special about being pregnant. There, I said it. Of course, I speak from personal experience. We were lucky. We had no problems on the whole fertility front, no medical issues. I braced for the inconveniences I had come to expect: weeks and months of mood swings, weight gain, the less-than-flattering wardrobe, the scheduled C-section.

I was, by then, over thirty-five, so my doctor recommended I have an amniocentesis—my first. The procedure concluded with certainty that the baby was a girl. But a sonogram the same day concluded, with equal certainty, that the baby was a boy. I've seen a lot of sonograms, and this baby was *definitely* a boy. I'll admit several days passed as I tried to come to terms with having a hermaphrodite baby—not that there is anything wrong with that!—until the hospital determined that there had been a typo somewhere between the test lab and my doctor's office: The "XY" was put in as an "XX." It was just human error, and they happen all the time, in all disciplines. Since I work in a field where human error can have grave consequences, I'm somewhat sympathetic to those who don't.

As I entered my third trimester, in late August 2005, a Category 5 hurricane slammed into the Gulf Coast. More than one thousand people died as a result of its devastation. The hurricane was horrible, of course, but the week that followed was worse. The levees in New Orleans that held the Gulf at bay broke in several places, spilling water throughout regions of the city. Response efforts were chaotic: city, state, and federal resources were delayed, evacuation efforts were disorganized, and people who did not need to die did.

Hurricane Katrina, and the government's response, proved what was so wrong with policies built around the ideology of "Never Again." Never again, what? As the levees broke, we realized that we had focused on preventing terrorism at the expense of our response and emergency management apparatuses. We were to unable to save a city from drowning. The challenges that New Orleans faced existed well before Hurricane Katrina—systemic poverty, public-sector incompetence, corrupt police, a neglected infrastructure, including levees that were known to be inadequate—especially for (lest we forget) a city that long ago was built below sea level. But the failures, at all levels of government, served as an important reminder that our focus on war had led us to abandon other responsibilities.

And those were the responsibilities of the Department of Homeland Security, the newest member of the federal family. Hurricane Katrina was, in many respects, DHS's first major moment in prime time. Could this agency deliver services and help when citizens needed it most? No, but not for all the obvious reasons. DHS was crippled from the start.

Opening its doors in 2003 under an administration that didn't actually want it, DHS combined twenty-two different agencies into the third-largest department in DC, behind the Departments of Defense and Veterans Affairs. Before DHS, President Bush maintained an Office of Homeland Security in the White House, which was led by Tom Ridge. For some time, Bush fought off calls from many Democrats to create a federal agency with the budget to match the homeland's needs. In their mind, a minor office in the bowels of the White House didn't have sufficient cachet. And, what's more, given the rules regarding White House personnel, Ridge was immune from oversight or congressional hearings. From a political perspective, this call for a big agency was a way for Democrats to show that they, too, were tough on terror.

And so Bush tapped a "Gang of Five," senior White House officials from the chief of staff's office and the National Security Council, to create some semblance of a department. With little input, and with no disclosure to the other cabinet secretaries, Bush's architects grabbed a little bit from here, stole a little bit from there, and announced a new department.

There was no rhyme or reason as to which agencies were chosen. Initially, there was no policy office set up to guide the department's planning, which is why its actions seemed random at some times, incomprehensible at others. The United States Secret Service, which protects the president and other VIPs, was now part of the department, but the Federal Aviation Administration, which protects the skies, was not. The Coast Guard was reassigned from the Treasury Department, but the National Guard remained in the Defense Department. They grabbed the Plum Island Animal Disease Center from the Department of Agriculture. The CIA and FBI, whose failures were well documented in post-9/11 reviews, remained as they were. The Department created its own surveillance entity, which would come to be known as the Office of Intelligence and Analysis. Yet just weeks before DHS was to hold its opening ceremony, the president announced that another entity—the National Counterterrorism Center—would lead all efforts in the war on terror. It was not placed at DHS.

The secrecy surrounding these plans meant that when the merger was finally announced, there was little enthusiasm from those who now reported to a new department. This was especially true of DHS's operating components.

DHS and the Pentagon share a similar organizational structure: the secretary and leadership teams in budget, procurement, policy, and communications guide the activities of large operational units. The Pentagon's military branches—the marines, army, navy, and air force—are deployed where needed. The same is true at DHS: Most of its two hundred thousand employees work at operational agencies like the

Transportation Security Administration, the Coast Guard, Citizenship and Immigration Services, Immigration and Customs Enforcement, Customs and Border Protection, the Federal Emergency Management Agency, and the Secret Service; they are deployed throughout the country, at our borders, airports, waterways, and cities and towns.

DHS's operational components stumbled: Airport screening was long and laborious. Immigration enforcement was performed heartlessly. DHS's leadership flailed, too: A color-code system to designate scary times from not-scary times was ridiculed and reviled. Once confirmed as the department's first secretary, Ridge struggled to even get an audience with his cabinet brethren.

DHS didn't even have a headquarters big enough to house all of its agencies. The Nebraska Avenue Complex, or NAC, is an old navy facility that looks like a small college campus. It sits across the street from American University in a suburban area of Washington, DC. The NAC housed only a small portion of DHS, which had more than thirty other offices throughout the DC region. The agencies that were melded into the department never even left their original homes. All of its major operational components, like FEMA and the Coast Guard, had headquarters miles away. If power is all about location, location, location, then DHS was too dispersed to assert any.

Like other agencies born from the ashes of trauma—such as the Energy Department, which emerged after the 1973 oil crisis—it could take decades for DHS to find its footing. It is no surprise, then, that all four DHS secretaries have entered their office demanding yet another strategic review to pave a way forward for DHS and its operational components.

The major DHS component in charge during Katrina was FEMA, once an independent authority with cabinet-level status. There is often a misconception about FEMA: Disaster strikes, and many envision FEMA, when it works, descending in vans, trucks, and helicopters, its forces fanning out to dispense aid. In fact, it is more of a coordination agency than an army. It only employs a couple thousand staffers. Instead, it works with various states throughout the homeland, which is divided up into ten different FEMA regions, to ensure that each understands what is required when disaster strikes. There are earthquakes and tsunamis in Region IX (which includes Hawaii and California), ice storms and hurricanes in Region I (New England). FEMA liaises with each state's emergency management agency, which in turn works with local emergency managers to assess needs on the ground. FEMA, therefore, can direct a great deal of expertise, resources, and money—including post-disaster relief—but it always stands in support of local and state involvement.

Here is how it works: Say you are the local emergency manager of a small Nevada town called Searchlight. Your town's needs tend to focus on heat waves, fire, and drought. One sunny June day, a nearby dam, a not atypical random piece of neglected infrastructure, breaks and starts flooding areas of your jurisdiction. You need, more than anything else, a bunch of helicopters to evacuate people stranded in isolated areas.

But you don't have helicopters. You barely have enough cars. After all, you are just some government employee in Searchlight, Nevada. So you call Nevada's state emergency management agency, which should—based on mutual aid agreements—be able to find and lend you helicopters from other local jurisdictions or, failing that, from the National Guard or state police. And if there aren't enough, Nevada's state emergency management agency calls over to Arizona to borrow some helicopters from their emergency management agencies.

Now let's just say that that dam is the Hoover Dam. The Hoover Dam is a really big dam, and the water behind it is the largest body of its kind in the United States. That would be bad. And you're just some emergency manager in a small town, and now need a *lot* of freaking helicopters, and the state is getting a whole bunch of phone calls from other emergency managers just like you who are screaming for helicopters right now because it's a matter of life and death and this is the Hoover Dam!

Well—if the Hoover Dam breaks, that means that the states surrounding Nevada are also flooded and in need of helicopters. And not just helicopters. There are requests for every other logistical asset: cars, ambulances, tents, bedding, water, water trucks, lights, first responders from every discipline, distribution centers, medical units, triage tents, shelter facilities for the elderly, shelter facilities for the young, shelter facilities for pets. Do not forget the pets: people love their dogs and cats and will actually die for them. Every sophisticated emergency management agency also has a plan for the pets.

So it's bad everywhere downstream from the Hoover Dam, so bad that no local or state government can deal with the mess. Enter FEMA, an agency that likely will have already placed individuals in the states' emergency operations centers to field requests for various commodities needed. A helicopter? Well, we happen to have an entire military with a bunch of those, and since we can't very well expect local emergency managers to call the Pentagon looking for a heli-copter, FEMA makes the request for them. Need a bunch of boats? FEMA calls the Coast Guard. How about measuring that water qual-ity? FEMA calls the Environmental Protection Agency (EPA). Need some radios? Turns out FEMA knows people at the Federal Commu-nications Commission. FEMA is much less like an army than it is like a Walmart of the federal government.

Admittedly, it's a little more technical than this. Terms like "emergency support functions" are used to describe the organization of fifteen categories of federal efforts, but you get the gist. You just want a helicopter. FEMA is supposed to get you one. And that is what it failed to do during Katrina.

What happened to FEMA in those early years was not preor-dained by its merger into DHS; agencies like the Coast Guard, for example, continued to flourish. I believe the real problem was that emergency management just didn't reflect the mood of the times. We focused on terrorism, and while hurricanes are bad, they aren't bad guys. To put it bluntly, FEMA wasn't about "Never Again."

For the counterterrorism, border, and intelligence specialists who staffed DHS in its early days, FEMA was an afterthought. Changes made to FEMA's docket in the early days of DHS were detrimental to its response efforts. The department diverted billions of dollars from FEMA that had once been allocated to states and localities for disaster prevention to DHS agencies focused on terrorism preven-tion, reassigning FEMA's responsibility to guide state and local plan-ning to another entity at DHS. And without the ability to administer funds, FEMA lost a tremendous amount of influence at the local and state levels. DHS was looking for a terrorist in every airplane; it had forgotten how powerful Mother Nature can be.

This neglect was, to a certain extent, Michael Brown's responsibility. He led FEMA up to and during the early days of Hurricane Katrina, and the quality of his performance as its director is a matter of considerable debate. Famously praised on television by President Bush, who liked to give nicknames to his team, with "Brownie, you're doing a heck of a job," Brown was fired by Bush a few days later. But blame for catastrophes like Hurricane Katrina is rarely rightly placed on a single villain's shoulders. Brown merely stands in a long line of folks bearing their portion of blame: Consider the fact that Brown's confirmation hearing, based on a rather lackluster career as the head of the International Arabian Horse Association, was only twenty-two minutes long. Not even the Senate viewed FEMA as worthy of the minutes we generally commit to a prime-time sitcom.

I knew Brown; he had been a member of one of the advisory groups we invited to the Kennedy School regularly. I found him formidable. It turns out that Brown's arrogance made him a force to reckon with at DHS, and I heard stories about how he tried to increase FEMA's presence and budget even as the department seemed to care less and less about the agency he oversaw. I suspect that he was well aware of FEMA's systemic limitations in the days leading up to Katrina. Frustrated and isolated at DHS, he had planned to announce his resignation just a few days before Katrina formed into a Category 5 hurricane.

As I sat at home, pregnant, watching water flood the streets of New Orleans, its citizens abandoned by its leaders, I was appalled. Government that was supposed to work clearly hadn't—the evidence was broadcast 24-7 on CNN. Like every mother watching that day, I felt that when a parent steals from an abandoned convenience store to get diapers and baby formula, it is not exactly looting. Technically it is, yes, but I prefer to call it parenting. Given my experiences during the day of 9/11 and the anthrax scare, I was inclined to be sympathetic to parents with children in harm's way.

There had to be a lesson here, I thought. Indeed, if you are a publicly declared disaster management expert, there's more than just one lesson to learn. Surely someone like me could make a plan to protect my family, unlike many of the people I saw on television, who were the victims of systemic poverty and likely had no resources. If I didn't try to prepare my family for something like this, or even something less than this, then I had failed as a security mom.

My self-help attitude, I am told, can at times seem slightly militant. I think that partially unfair. Rather, it grows from a notion that citizens should take some responsibility for their safety, especially those who have the resources to act responsibly. I often begin public speeches with a quiz: how many in the audience, I ask, have a plan for protecting themselves in the case of an emergency? What about protecting their families? Invariably, only a few people raise their hands, and so I then spend a couple of minutes berating everybody else: If they have the time to attend keynote addresses and board meetings, surely they have the time to prepare themselves for disaster.

"What are you waiting for?" I ask. "You got this."

Nearly eight months pregnant, I was not addressing audiences as a keynote speaker. I did, however, have a few words for parents at our day care facility.

The Botanic Gardens Children's Center sits on a faculty housing–lined street near the Radcliffe Quadrangle and right next to Harvard University Press. A single-story building adjacent to a big playground, its hallways are adorned with cheerful renderings of scenes from favorite children's books. Its clientele is varied; over the years, I met researchers from Russia, an Italian couple with a journalism fellowship, a Chinese lab technician who arrived with a wife and three non-English-speaking kids in tow (all of whom managed to start reading their second language before any of mine mastered their first), and young faculty parents like David and me who came to rely on day care.

We loved that our young children were surrounded by such a diverse crowd. It proved to be a great experiment in germ sharing and, as they got older, a source of never-ending fart jokes (in multiple languages!). Though we often relied on a nanny or student babysitter when day care or school hours didn't match our normal work schedules, when Cecilia and Leo turned one, off to day care they went. Our yet-to-be-born youngest son, Jeremiah, would soon follow.

Hurricane Katrina gave me a mission. It was summer, so I was already on leave from teaching. A few days after the levees collapsed, I set about rummaging through our basement to see whether I could pass my own test. I have always been a Costco and Target fan. Over the years, I've had the habit of buying extras of everything: ketchup, bottled water, paper towels, Diet Coke, plastic trash bags, toilet paper, and Ziploc bags. I would randomly buy various items to cover our bases. But my purchasing behavior wasn't exactly organized around a "be ready" mantra.

It turns out I had a lot more than I thought: there was plenty of water, baby food and formula, dried fruit and Gatorade, fruit snacks and Pepto-Bismol. (Diarrhea, after all, is one of the most prevalent forms of easily curable illness; left unchecked, it can lead to dehydration.) There were flashlights and batteries, candles and matches, and items any frequent Costco shopper buys, because we all think we absolutely need a five-gallon jar of trail mix and sixty-four granola bars. There were diapers, lots of diapers, but then again I had two children under five and was expecting another.

Once I mastered the basement, I attacked the paperwork. I wanted an accounting of all our important documents, to know what I had and what I needed to protect, lest something happen to the house. That, too, wasn't as bad as I remembered. I made big files marked "Cecilia," "Leo," and "TBD," and stacked paperwork accordingly. As I sorted, I organized their birth certificates and Social Security cards, mailed copies to my parents and in-laws out of state (since storing the copies next to the originals doesn't help much), and put the cleaned-up files in a safe and isolated area.

I also hid cash. An envelope of tens and twenties is always stashed in my house, its whereabouts unknown to my husband. I realize this is somewhat unfair to him—what, after all, should happen if disaster finds him holding down the fort alone? But David's sister told me at our wedding that our marriage would last if I never responded when David began a question with: "Have you seen my . . . ?" He has a tendency to leave his wallet or car keys in places that don't make much sense. I didn't want to let accessible cash be a crutch.

Looking back, I can see how my activities during that long, hot

August constituted a type of nesting, a familiar chore for those preparing to welcome a new child. Of course, with my first two children, I was inspired to perform all sorts of housekeeping tasks in advance of their arrival. But with my last, with the TV playing news about Hurricane Katrina as I moved about the house, my preparation differed slightly. Is this how security moms nest? Possibly. While my organizational skills, focus, and preparation took on epic proportions, they sounded somewhat familiar to friends who had also waited sleepless nights for their babies to arrive. Nesting, but with some knowledge and some serious oomph. I knew, from my experience with the anthrax scare, that should disaster strike, we would want to bunker down, safe, with our children at home.

I was living the "Be Ready" dream, big time. I knew that sh-t happens.

But now that I was confident my family would be safe at home, I turned my attention to the places where we spent many hours of our days. David and I both worked nearby while our kids were at day care. If our phones didn't work, we could walk to fetch them. But if we couldn't make it there, what would happen? I analyzed the day care's preparation plans in my head: they had a fire drill occasionally, but in a real crisis it wasn't clear where people would go, whether our kids could leave with someone else, or if staying put would be a good idea.

I volunteered as the room parent for Leo's class and served as the day care board's representative for Cecilia's class—to compensate, I guess, for putting the children in day care, and for the occasional travel that kept me away from home; I recommend such positions to anyone with strong opinions about milk (whole or skim? organic?) and the weather (if properly dressed, what temperature is too cold for kids to play outside?). It's also a huge responsibility to deal with teacher salaries, health benefits, and the physical management of a place that looks after your own children. It means asking tough questions.

When the day care reopened that first week in September, I had the toughest one on my mind.

"What is the plan?" I said. The flooding continued in Louisiana, and the drowned city was on everyone's minds. "We should not expect the government to take care of us at every moment. There's so much we can do now."

The director of the facility talked about fire drills and locking doors. It wasn't the answer I was looking for, but I feared that if I discussed what I knew from my experience as a homeland security expert, I would sound a little paranoid. I asked anyway. I needed to make sure my kids would be safe.

"Given what is going on with Katrina," I began, "and that our kids are here all day, do we have a sense of how things would unfold, or how they ought to unfold, in the event of a disaster?" I paused. Although I had asked these questions before, without hesitation, in a professional capacity, this felt different. I pressed on. "Do the parents know what they should do? I mean," I remember saying, with all sorts of "um"s and awkward efforts at smiles, "what is the plan if something *really bad* happened?" I looked around. The outer halls were decorated with our children's art. Most rooms had chairs too small for an adult to sit in. Paint-splattered smocks hung from a peg near a bank of easels sized for midgets and five-year-olds. Brightly colored books were arrayed front covers out—a very hungry caterpillar beside a pigeon eager to drive a bus. In that setting, just raising the question seemed unnatural. Judging by the faces of my fellow board members, they thought so, too.

I charged on, offering to write a memo detailing what I believed every parent should do to prepare for a major disaster, including how to ready their homes and the day care. How could anyone in that room say no? I was the expert—the security mom of security moms. This wasn't pure altruism. Jeremiah was due in a few weeks, and he, too, would be heading to Botanic eventually.

The resulting document was sent home with finger paintings, a back-to-school meeting announcement, and a flu-shot information memo. It might best be described as the day care's normal fire drill procedures on steroids. In it I advised that parents should work together to determine the answers to a few questions. They're worth repeating here because they remain relevant, whether your kids attend Botanic Gardens or another school:

- Assuming that cell phone service is out, how best will you communicate with your family and the day care?
- Assuming public transportation and roads are not usable, how best will you get to the school to pick up your child(ren)?
- Are alternative guardians known to the school and your child? Are they knowledgeable about your plan?
- If you travel, is the school aware of where you are at all times?

- Do you have copies of essential documents? Are those copies mailed to others out of state?

- Do backup family members know their role in your plan?

- If storage and resources allow, do you have extra provisions of water, food, batteries, and diapers in your home?

- When was the last time you looked at your first aid kit provisions? Do you have a first aid kit?

- If you have a backup place to stay, is it also ready with these provisions?

Exactly what I expected the parents' collective response would be, I cannot recall. But I knew that, should disaster strike, any parent's primary objective would be holding our children in our arms as quickly as possible. There is no other goal. As parents, we know that at our core, but we spend too little time thinking about how to make that happen if things go, well, badly. It was time we talked about it.

I figured most of the parents would throw the document in the trash. I expected my friends to laugh. I wondered if a few of those friends would ask how much longer I had to wait until Jeremiah was born, as then I'd be less prone to take on side projects. But I didn't expect hostility. It threw me.

"Don't you think this is overkill?" one parent asked me via e-mail.

"This is pretty inappropriate," remarked another, as if the kids were actually reading the list.

And, echoing the "Keep Calm" mantra, one father had the nerve to say: "At this stage in the pregnancy, I think you can start drinking wine. Or at least take a chill pill."

I could understand how these parents might want to delegate responsibility for their security. With the memory of 9/11 looming, with Katrina flooding the Gulf Coast, with wars being waged and threat levels escalating on the nightly news, perhaps these parents felt—like many others—unprepared to tackle a problem of such magnitude, a challenge of such scope. It wasn't their problem.

They were parents who worried about skinned knees and solo bike rides; not necessarily parents who worried about mayhem and flooding. They had divided the home from the homeland. I had unwittingly put the reality of their own responsibility in a memo and shoved it down their throats. Yet I was glad I had. Parents who practice the habits of grip, moms and dads who have a plan, make for more resilient citizens, the building blocks of a resilient country.

That it had come to this—my shoving and their hostility—reflected how the government had failed on many fronts. I understood that, to many, any talk of homeland security in a liberal town like Cambridge, Massachusetts, meant—somehow—buying into Bush's agenda. It was as if the fact of reading my memo signified their acquiescence to his administration's use of waterboarding. Homeland security, and the department that oversaw it, were Republican creations. They were the products of a post-9/11 attitude, one in which we seemed to have lost our way. Perhaps these parents believed the submerged city of New Orleans was just another data point, showing us how far we had strayed. I get that.

But I also knew that it was a completely self-defeating attitude. If anything, Hurricane Katrina should have alerted us to the necessity of taking our own security—in the home, and in the homeland—seriously. Government can fail, miserably. We all saw it. Our families' needs should not be sacrificed to make a political or spiritual point. We don't need to live in fear of catastrophic disaster striking at any time. Preparedness means taking responsibility in the event that it might. When more people are prepared, fewer people will need help. That will minimize the possibility of greater catastrophe.

If you've ever flown on an airplane, you've been introduced to the concept: in case of a loss of cabin pressure, you first secure your own oxygen mask before assisting those around you. It can be jarring to hear that admonition. It rests on the fundamental premise that those who can help themselves and do so will actually help those who cannot.

Scale up that idea to a full-blown disaster. We need to reserve precious government resources for those who can't help themselves: children, the old, the infirm, the poor, and those who find themselves in the wrong place at the wrong time. If everyone is calling 911 in a panic, then government has limited capacity to focus on who really needs help. If the response is focused, made so because the vast majority of the public has taken some responsibility for their own security, society can begin to recover sooner. It can bounce back faster.

Here's the funny thing: almost all of us already understand the need for basic planning, even if we haven't quite prepared for a disaster. As parents, we plan all the time. We don't buy laundry detergent every time we need to do the laundry; we keep more than one Band-Aid in the medicine cabinet; we shop for school clothes when they're on sale, weeks before the kids will need them; we choreograph dozens of drop-offs and pickups at soccer fields, judo classes, piano lessons—you name it; we manage to oversee most homework getting done on time, even those long-lead projects like the family tree and the dry-ice volcano. If you like golf, odds are you have spare golf balls; if your thing is cooking, odds are you've got a stocked pantry; if your passion is fixing cars, odds are you've got a toolbox to shame a mechanic. We get preparedness. Home security is easy. Applying those skills to homeland security would be, too, if we were simply shown how.

I hoped some day-care families, after reading my instructions, took heed. We live in a world where tornados strike and terrorists plot. Planning for it need not be scary. If anything, it can be empowering, as it is in many other areas of our lives. Make a list. Talk to your kids. Check the first aid kit. Hoard some groceries, if you can. Think through the contingencies. Copy those essential documents. Share your plans with family members. These are the habits of grip.

And I would need a huge dose of it. Jeremiah was born in October 2005. With three kids, David and I were outnumbered. It was a little overwhelming at first, but finally we got into a groove. I went back to the Kennedy School and traveled some for consulting and board work, and though our personal life was anything but calm, with David and I passing each other in the driveway on most weekends as we went from soccer to gymnastics with our children, it was stable.

Just a year after Jeremiah was born, I resigned from the Botanic day care board. My schedule didn't permit it any longer. That groove that David and I had worked so hard to maintain was about to change, once again, as I accepted a position with our soon-to-be governor—and my former boss—Deval Patrick. I was trading in toy fire trucks and bulk purchases of crayons for a totally different kind of equipment.

THE ART OF DISASTER MANAGEMENT

IN EARLY 2006, DEVAL PATRICK, MY OLD BOSS FROM THE CIVIL RIGHTS DIVISION of the Justice Department, visited David and me at our home to discuss his professional plans. I was nursing Jeremiah. David was taking a semester off on paternity leave. We had just invested in a selection of manlier baby accessories, like a diaper bag from Patagonia.

Patrick was making a run for governor of Massachusetts—and he wanted our help. I have always admired Patrick. David and I first heard him speak when we were still law students; he argued passionately against the death penalty. "Who is he?" I had said to David, amazed at his energy and compassion, as well as the artfulness of his oration. Later, as my boss at the Civil Rights Division, he gave me incredible latitude in my cases, letting me bring a new type of civil rights harassment complaint for peer-on-peer hazing. And while we didn't run in the same circles but both called Boston home, we occasionally met in the years after the Clinton presidency.

His candidacy seemed improbable at the time. An African-American lawyer from the south side of Chicago, he was running against a party establishment that had aligned around the sitting attorney general. But David and I were huge fans.

We promised our support while we ate Caesar salads that Patrick had picked up from a restaurant down the street. When I excused myself to go nurse Jeremiah, I heard David ask: "We're all in, but how are you going to do this?"

Patrick had been working for over a year to secure support and delegates in the state's primary caucus system. Quietly, he appealed to those who believed that the country needed better leadership. He made a clear reference to the infamous Hurricane Katrina picture of President Bush flying over tragedy-stricken New Orleans, looking down from ten thousand feet above: "I would get off the plane," he said.

Patrick won the nomination. He had done the improbable. We held a fund-raiser and invited more of our friends to join the campaign. After a bruising general election battle against the sitting lieutenant governor, a woman who might have been the first female governor of Massachusetts, Patrick became our governor.

As Patrick put his team in place in late 2006 and early 2007, he asked me to consult on the major homeland security issues facing the commonwealth. So I went to a few meetings and wrote a couple of memos, which included my thoughts on topics as diverse as our nuclear power facility and how to better utilize homeland security funds coming to the state to support our first responders. Most significantly,

Patrick needed a homeland security advisor. The federal government required that each state appoint one; in an emergency, this person would be the single point of contact for DHS. In addition, the homeland security advisor would supervise strategic preparedness planning, advise on the distribution of federal funds to first responders, work with communities on responding to all threats, and oversee the state's National Guard.

When Patrick asked if I was interested, I said yes without a moment's thought. I believed in him and I wanted to help, in the field instead of in the ivory tower. I was ready to jump back into government work. This time, though, I had three children.

Logistically, I hoped that directing Massachusetts's homeland security would be challenging but manageable: the state was geographically compact, the public safety community relatively small, and the threats knowable. What I couldn't imagine was how difficult my family's schedule would become. Working long hours while parenting three kids under six was a logistical nightmare. We had day-care drop-off, a nanny in the afternoon to help with pickup, Stop & Shop deliveries at ten p.m. when we couldn't make it to the market, and endless soccer games and birthday parties each weekend. As a parent, it is only when you get out of that stage—what I call the "gear" stage, when you always leave the house with bags in tow—that you recognize its intensity. It was a good week if I could find the time to run a few miles and grab coffee with a girlfriend.

The announcement of my appointment after Patrick's inauguration in January 2007 wouldn't have been particularly notable except that I was the first Arab-American to serve as a governor's homeland security advisor. I get why it's a story. The newspapers would never admit why they found it worthy of mention, but I always sensed some skepticism in the press—it was as if a fox were guarding the henhouse. Despite my years of expertise, I still had to prove myself.

The public nature of this position was new to both David and me. Once, the *Boston Globe* sent a photographer to our house for a feature story. While he uploaded a picture of me from his car in our driveway, David came home. David yelled at the photographer, demanding to know why he had a picture of me. I don't know what David was planning to do next, but I do love that man.

Some parts of this position felt new; others, familiar. Luckily, I already knew my way to the statehouse, and to Ashburton Place, where I worked, just a few miles from home. And, of course, I was once again tasked with completing clearance papers. In the post-9/11 world, I was grateful that I only had to update my previous clearance. The process was lengthier this time, more rigorous and onerous. Again, there were lots of questions about my family from Lebanon, but I passed.

On my first day in office, I introduced myself to public safety teams in the state police, the Department of Fire Services, the Massachusetts Emergency Management Agency, and the National Guard. I would come to depend on these men and women. My job required that I manage the state's homeland security planning by supporting their efforts. This was no easy task, as the role cut across almost every agency imaginable—public health, transportation, public safety, and local efforts in our state's 351 cities and towns—and often with little direct-line authority.

I also supervised the National Guard, which reports to the

governor's office. The National Guard is an integral part of any state's security efforts, though most of its members are part-time volunteers. I imagine that the generals of the National Guard had some opinions about reporting directly to me, a thirty-six-year-old lawyer by training. But the military's insistence on the chain of command meant that I heard none of it. I suspect that my tendency to swear and my ability to outpace many of them on the track (I once showed up to a new-recruit training session in running gear for the competition) eased some of their concerns. I was honored by the respect the National Guard showed me; it went both ways. I was devastated by the frequency with which I was asked to attend farewell ceremonies and funerals for men and women deployed to fight in Iraq and Afghanistan.

In addition to the day-to-day activities of the position, I was also required to prepare for the unexpected. Simply put, when sh-t happened, I had to be there. As I had done when I was pregnant, I prepared a "go bag"—although it contained slightly different items. I packed a change of work clothes, sweats, a laminated list of all essential work phone numbers, and a few water bottles and PowerBars. I stashed it near the front door. I was given a satellite phone that would work if communications systems were down. I was handed a law enforcement badge. I was fitted with military boots. I was once again equipped with a lot of new gear; it just wasn't strollers and diaper bags anymore. And then there was the car.

The car, I should note, wasn't just any car. I was issued a state police cruiser with sirens and unexplainable gizmos on the dashboard. There are no other words for it—it was really, really cool. It was authorized for personal use, so its backseat was filled with kids' car seats and a fine dusting of snack crumbs. A strange juxtaposition: sirens in the front and cheetah-print baby seats in the back.

I was given the car as a necessity; it wasn't a perk but a precaution. My job was to deal with the consequences of a bad blizzard, a big fire, or an impending hurricane on the Cape, and if I was needed somewhere, I had to get there. The car was sturdy enough to withstand high winds, mounds of snow, and, wouldn't you know, three kids yelling in the back.

The car came in handy in early 2007, as I prepared for my first crisis in office. A major winter storm was on the horizon. I had to help direct the state's response to the news. With every storm, there is a tendency—particularly in local news media—to pretend as if we have never seen snow before. A certain hysteria becomes part of the narrative: people rush to the grocery stores, hoard salt, and act as if snow—*snow!*—has never fallen from the sky. Every year, the newspaper questions whether the neighbor who has shoveled out his car and reserved his now-vacant spot with a few chairs has acted within his rights. As a public safety official, I had to denounce the practice. As a parent living in a part of Cambridge with precious little street parking, I had other views.

That morning, all of the leaders of the public safety teams, as well as the governor, arrived at the Massachusetts Emergency Management Agency (MEMA). MEMA is hidden underground, off Route 9, in the sprawling Boston suburb of Framingham. It is a bunker, and that is what we called it. It is a legacy of Massachusetts's favorite son President John F. Kennedy's domestic preparedness program. In 1961, Kennedy became a strong proponent of community sheltering capacity, well before the Cuban missile crisis. "It is insurance that we trust will never be needed," he said, "but insurance which we could never forgive ourselves for forgoing in the event of a catastrophe." He conducted a federal inventory of shelters and focused on where there were gaps. His initiative led to the establishment of state emergency management bunkers throughout the country, including the one built in his home state in Framingham. A plaque dedicated to him is still displayed in the windowless hallway of MEMA.

In the bunker's emergency operations center, one big-screen television delivers news while others show maps of potential flooding or traffic conditions. It looks a little like NASA's mission control, but on a state budget. Rows of tables all face the main screen. Various first-responder personnel sit at designated incident command areas on the main floor, their duties heralded by signs hanging from the ceiling: logistics, transportation, supplies, budget, sheltering, public affairs, etcetera.

From this main area in the center of the bunker, corridors stretch out to smaller rooms reserved for particular functions and, as needed, for private discussions. The governor would often be briefed in one of these rooms, or prepare there with his staff for a press conference. Down one long corridor is a Soviet-style cafeteria, where cholesterol-heavy food is served. They even have Twinkies. Tucked at the end of another hallway are sleeping and shower rooms, used when we stayed at the bunker overnight. And finally, in the back, there are multiple generators and electrical sources should anyone need to stay for a long, long time.

The threat of this storm meant that it wasn't just the cops or emergency managers who came to the bunker. Subway transportation experts, the guys who monitor the Massachusetts Turnpike, representatives from our major airports, and members of the secretary of education's team, as well as private-sector leaders who had a say in the management of major infrastructure in the state, all met in the large emergency operations room.

This had the potential to be a big storm.

Governor Patrick arrived at MEMA to assess the choices ahead and question his team. This was his approach: ask a lot of questions, and then decide. No looking back. As we sat there weighing the decisions we had to make to protect citizens, there was a single pressing issue that had to be settled first. It cuts to the core of how we function as a society, who we are as a nation, and how much we love our children:

Would the state advise a snow day?

In the same way that the federal government liaises with fifty unruly states, each state coordinates with a bunch of unruly cities and local jurisdictions, each with its own mayor or county commissioner or *someone* in charge. The state cannot force a district to close its schools, for example, but it can make a strong recommendation in light of the superior knowledge the state possesses about the crisis. That day, we convened to decide what we would suggest to local jurisdictions and the public about closures. The decision to close schools inevitably causes a trickle-down effect, as employees stay home to parent the kids who've been told to stay home. Local businesses feel the impact. It is an important, and expensive, decision to make.

Let me just make this clear: I love my children—I do. My

inclination, as a mother, is always to protect them. But this decision required that we weigh subjective analysis and specific but sometimes inconclusive information. We assessed the accuracy of a weather-monitoring system that predicted the storm's impact, the likelihood of the snow blocking streets or screwing up travel, and the speed with which emergency agencies could clean up the mess. Would my children be safer at home? Would everyone's children be safer at home?

And I was the only woman, let alone mother, at the long table. If the fathers at the table were fighting the same internal wrestling match in their heads as I was, I didn't know it.

Team Don't Close: If my kids stay home, if we are to head in that direction, it is just the beginning of a double whammy for me. First, there is work. Closing schools is not done often in New England. When it happens, it means that things are serious. I am likely to be staying in the bunker for a stretch of time. And it also means that my kids will be home, their day care or school closed, which means I've got a whole other series of calibrations to make. Can David cover care, and for how long? Is the storm hitting on a day our babysitter has her college classes? Can she even make it to our house safely? What about the refrigerator? Is there enough milk and food? When was the last time I checked the flashlight batteries? Did I ever replace the kids' snow gloves that were lost during last month's storm? Why do my kids always lose their gloves? Is it me?

Team Close: What if we are wrong and we minimize the forecasts and children are put in danger?

I was on Team Close. Given the predictions, we couldn't risk the gamble.

The governor went around the room, asking everyone their opinions. Everyone. In these situations, Patrick is all business. He has a way of looking over his glasses, chin down, and pegging his team with questions in a way that could make us feel like plagiarizing students being questioned by a headmaster. He turned to Michael Coelho, the secretary of public safety's chief of staff.

"What do you think?" the governor asked Coelho.

Coelho is a master planner, perfect in the role of chief of staff, but the governor's question made him nervous. "Who the hell cares what I think?" he later said to me. Still, Coelho had replied bluntly: close it down.

There was near unanimity that we would let state employees go home early, given that the snow was coming in around three p.m., set to hit maximum flurry after eight p.m., and dump over a foot of snow through four a.m.

"Okay, let's do this," the governor said. A well-honed response apparatus went into action. Notifications were sent throughout the state, agencies deployed additional resources, volunteers geared up for snow removal, and schools sent the kids home and told them to stay home. The decision we made in the bunker was a green light for the public safety teams to do what they train for every day: protecting communities and people.

Every emergency response begins at the most local level. Each city and town has its own response plan based on population, resources, geography, and the particular needs of the community. Only a local community knows where the senior-citizen homes are located; only it understands the linguistic needs of an immigrant population.

The basic building block of homeland security is, first, the home, and right after that, the hometown.

The state is the next block, deploying its own resources to support local needs (and deficiencies), protecting state highways and toll roads, and coordinating messaging. Through MEMA, it provides localities access to more gear, equipment, and personnel, including the National Guard if needed. Behind that, and always present at our meetings at MEMA, is the federal effort represented by FEMA.

The governor addressed the media in a conference room at the bunker. He put on a MEMA fleece vest to reflect his confidence in the response teams, a vest that over the course of his eight years in office he wore through Hurricane Sandy, several serious blizzards, and a terrorist attack on the Boston Marathon. That vest became a symbol of his governorship not simply because he wore it but because of how often it seemed he needed to wear it.

Luckily, I had my car that day and quickly returned to my office downtown—lights on, siren off—about a twenty-minute drive from MEMA's bunker, with Coelho in the passenger seat. That commute is a strategic design feature: The emergency management center should not be located in the middle of the state's biggest urban target. I never understood why, even after the terrorist attack in 1993, New York's emergency management agency was placed in the Twin Towers. It was destroyed on 9/11.

I called David at work on the drive home. He would deal with the crowds at the market, get gas, and take his books and grading home. He was prepared to stay there with the kids, since the day care, heeding our advice, had already closed for the next morning. We all have backup plans for any contingency. David, in so many ways, has always been mine.

As three p.m. rolled around, the skies were a stunning blue. Three fifteen, three thirty, and four p.m. passed without even a light dusting of snow. By five o'clock, the weather forecasts had shifted. The gloomy morning assessments had been revised based on some scientific calculation of wind and precipitation. The voices on the phone from the National Weather Service were annoyingly upbeat as they explained that Boston and the surrounding areas would no longer encounter any accumulation of snow. Having made certain decisions—letting state employees out at three p.m., issuing the school advisory—I wasn't as upbeat.

I came out of my office. Coelho stood in the main conference room, staring out the large floor-to-ceiling windows that overlooked downtown Boston and the harbor. His forehead was pressed against the windows. "Snow, dammit. *Snow!*" he said.

This is how it works, I thought. We were a group of experts making calls based on judgment. This isn't to say that we make it up as we go along; there is a plan. But the plan is guided as much by the facts and experience as it is by some organizational chart that often looks different in the cold light of day, or in this case, the clear skies of five p.m. The governor took full responsibility for the decision, even as he faced a media swarm that has little tolerance for mistakes. Coelho may have aged a few years that day, but he knew, as we all did, that there would be future guesses to make.

We made a judgment call based on what we knew. We were wrong. We would do better. Regroup, pivot, and learn. We had made a decision that it was better to be safe than sorry. It's not a bad mantra; I abide by it pretty regularly at home, as I believe we all should.

I spent that night at my house, monitored our response to the minimal accumulation from my cell phone, and tried to think of activities to keep the kids occupied, since their schools and day care were canceled. Oh yes, and David pivoted as well. He went into work the next morning. As he kissed me goodbye, I secretly cursed the team that had left me outnumbered three to one back at home.

ACCEPTABLE LOSSES AND BLACK SWANS

HOMELAND SECURITY: A DYSFUNCTIONAL COLOR-CODE SYSTEM, A HOLIER-THAN- thou approach to policy debates, a brutal airline security system that seemed to waste everyone's time. I felt that it was just lacking a certain touch: mine. Now that my team and I were on the inside, the department's struggles would miraculously disappear. Under our keen guidance, the state would spend money wisely, prepare sufficiently, and face every crisis with total competency.

Of course, it wasn't that easy.

The best analogies to describe my job as homeland security advisor weren't found in briefing memos or public policy papers, but in the books I read to my kids each night when I got home from work. Judith Viorst's *Alexander and the Terrible, Horrible, No Good, Very Bad Day* when disaster or an emergency struck, which reminded me that things could get better tomorrow. L. Frank Baum's *The Wonderful Wizard of Oz* when President Bush's Department of Homeland Security issued a raised terror alert with few details, leaving us to guess just what in fact the "wizard" knew. Shel Silverstein's *The Giving Tree* when I distributed necessary public funds to agencies throughout the state, giving and giving and giving until I had nothing more to give. But perhaps my favorite lesson came from "Goldilocks and the Three Bears": sometimes, just like Goldilocks, I kept searching for the "just right," that secure place between aggression ("too hot") and passivity ("too cold").

In 2007, when I entered state government, I inherited a security apparatus that was "too hot." In so many ways, we hadn't changed our thinking about homeland security since 9/11, even though we now had new technology and new intelligence that demanded we do so. But we didn't. Indeed, in the first few weeks of Governor Patrick's administration, our post-9/11 "too hot" security apparatus proved unwieldy.

On January 31, 2007, a driver spotted a large metallic box dangling off a well-traveled bridge. The strange contraption had exposed wires of unknown purpose. Similar devices were seen on critical infrastructure throughout the city. The Boston police responded to what looked like a bomb. Within a few hours, the entire area had come to a standstill, city and state resources had been deployed—including helicopters and bomb-sniffing dogs—and Mayor Tom Menino and Governor Patrick each addressed the public from the emergency center at the Boston Police Department.

And for the first time, I activated my own personal crisis plan, one that other parents in the field had recommended I arrange. They had reminded me that when sh-t happened, I would want a way to ensure that my own kids would be safe so I could focus on the job at hand.

David and I decided that Cara, our babysitter, would be our first phone call in an emergency, as she would likely be with the kids during the day. Cara had worked with us for a few months and was already a part of our family. When I first met her, I could see that she was more organized, and more patient, than me. (Reader, I hired her.) We knew that Cara would expertly take care of the kids, navigating the schools, the playdates, the meals, the social plans, whatever was on the list, while Mom was stuck in the bunker.

Actually, I was above ground, at the police department. CNN and other national networks were televising the "attack" live. It was anything but. Failures in communication between the bomb squad, which had already assessed that the devices were harmless, and the rest of the city led to a response that couldn't be stopped once it started. More cops, more dogs, more helicopters—more and more shows of force. Way too hot; way too hot.

It turned out that the devices had been placed around Boston by the Cartoon Network as a guerilla ad campaign for *Aqua Teen Hunger Force*, an animated TV show. The boxes—LED placards—were supposed to portray two glowing characters giving the middle finger to the unknowing masses. The Cartoon Network waited too long to take responsibility—they must have seen what was going on in Boston, yet failed to contact us—so we eventually demanded a couple million dollars to pay for the extra public safety costs they'd generated.

An executive vice president resigned within a week. Maybe we got to wave the last middle finger after all.

I realized then that this job was going to be harder than I imagined—and the Cartoon Network wasn't exactly to blame. It wasn't about incompetency or dereliction of duty. What was clear that day, and almost every day since, is that this nation has no good way of explaining risk, no vocabulary for how to calibrate harm. We know how to show force when a crisis demands it, but we're not very good at assessing the level of force required.

There had to be a better way. In a state like ours, built on progressive ideals, we could try to experiment with the security apparatus in ways that made sense. With a tremendous amount of support from a wildly popular governor who could afford to expend some equity on new policies, I tried to reassess our post-9/11 state, make changes, organize, and plan. Maybe I should have taken baby steps, but instead I went for the big one: the state's only nuclear power plant.

In the early days after 9/11, the police presence, and even the military presence, throughout the states was profound. Critical infrastructure sites like airports, bridges, electrical grids, ports, mass-transit systems, and telecommunications centers received extra security attention. If any of these critical infrastructure sites were destroyed or damaged, the consequences would impact whole swaths of the state and region.

Some history is in order. On September 12, 2001, then acting governor of Massachusetts Jane Swift assessed the state's security. Two of the airplanes involved in the attacks had taken off from Logan Airport in Boston, and many of the fatalities on those planes were

Commonwealth residents. It was personal here in a way that was different from most other places except New York and Washington, DC.

Like most governors, Swift faced uncertain terrain. There was no Department of Homeland Security to guide planning; there wasn't yet even a point person to contact at the White House. Planes were grounded and would stay that way for at least a few more days. The Massachusetts State Police and local police departments, especially in Boston, were on high alert as investigators identified the hijackers and tracked how they had spent their time in the city. A "temporary" security measure, instituted in October 2001 by Governor Swift, placed the exterior of the Pilgrim Nuclear Power Station under the protection of the Massachusetts National Guard.

That temporary solution was still in place in 2007.

By then, there was little justification for a National Guard presence. The facility was already highly fortified; it was not a soft target. Even if someone had infiltrated the facility, it would be almost impossible to do any serious damage. The time and skill needed to activate a nuclear meltdown that would cause serious harm is almost impossible to acquire. Take it from me, the terrorism expert: If you are a terrorist and you want to cause harm in the easiest way imaginable, getting into a nuclear facility is at the very bottom of your list. A terrorist wants ease of access without many security barriers. This is why the "soft targets"—places that are public and accessible—are favored by those who would do harm: places like major intersections, amusement parks, or hotels. Accidents, of course, are another matter, as Japan would realize a few years later. But no battery of weapons would do as much harm to a nuclear plant as a tsunami or, worse, human negligence. (The owners of the Pilgrim facility would, years later, announce its closure due to safety concerns related to the facility's construction and persistent maintenance challenges; terrorism did not factor into their decision.)

Yet twenty National Guard members still roamed the plant's perimeter. Housed in a temporary shelter a few feet from the entrance, they provided an aura of fortified security, but they had no tangible responsibilities. Worse, they gave all involved a false sense of invulnerability. The rare sort of threat that could actually pose a danger to the nuclear power plant was not the sort twenty soldiers could stop. Not a single person—Republican or Democrat, within the governor's office or without—would defend the guard's presence. And yet it remained.

It was bad policy. It cost way too much money, but the politics of changing it proved difficult. In America, and in any democracy, politics and security are always inextricably linked. We elect our mayors and governors under the assumption that they have our local interests in mind, that they will secure for us a level of safety that is consistent with those interests. Local leaders, after all, should have a better sense of what their communities need.

This community had come to depend on seeing these National Guard members outside the plant's perimeter. As they were likely unfamiliar with, and even unaware of, the layers and layers of preexisting security and fail-safes, those twenty guards became shorthand for, "I, my kids, my home—we're safe." Correspondingly, waking up to find them gone one morning would suggest the opposite. Their absence would be noticed.

Neither the public nor public safety officials could envision a less costly and more meaningful approach to the plant's security. We experts hadn't done our job: we hadn't provided alternative visions of homeland security; we hadn't discussed the kind of security they needed to keep their neighborhood, which happened to be near a nuclear reactor, safe.

I saw a way, by ending the program, of making Pilgrim and Plymouth, the community around the plant, safer. I was thinking like a mother. I imagined kids crossing streets, running after a stray baseball. I imagined the distracted drivers on those streets. I imagined the trick-or-treaters on Halloween, the hundreds of parents and children moving door to door in costume. Then I imagined twenty men with guns, in very large military vehicles, walking through that same residential neighborhood. I was paralyzed by the thought of a Humvee hitting some kid on a bike as it turned the corner, or a guardsman shooting an old retiree mistaken for a suicide bomber. Between the remote but extant threat of the nuclear facility being attacked and the reality of the armed military presence in a kids' play area, I had plenty to keep me up at night.

Any change in Plymouth required that my team exert its powers of persuasion. The area actively participated in local homeland security efforts, and its state senator, Therese Murray, served as the president of the senate at the statehouse. Her support would be crucial to the governor's overall plans for the state. She could not be easily ignored. Neither her office nor anyone in the community had any notion that we wanted to end the National Guard program at Pilgrim.

When we first broached the subject, community members and

their state legislators answered uniformly: "No way." They had come to rely on the presence of the soldiers. Plus, the federal government wasn't demanding the change. We pressed on, despite the political headache it would cause.

I won't deny that the new governor wanted to make a statement. The lessons of the Cartoon Network incident weighed on all of us. We had seen the ease with which a massive governmental response to a non-threat shut down Boston and much of the state. As we moved forward, we had to figure out a way to reflect the state's desire to protect its citizens without succumbing to fear. Progressive federalism, after all, is the notion that states, and not the federal government, should have leeway to establish their own democratic norms for the people they govern. This is the idea that has animated progress in arenas as diverse as gay marriage and immigration rights. While undeniably part of a federal security apparatus, our state—progressive in the best sense of the word—had every reason to try a new approach to security: one that was smarter, leaner, and less, as Goldilocks might say, "hot."

We were convinced change would make Plymouth safer. On reviewing the National Guard's program, we realized that new outside lighting, a more streamlined communications system between the plant and local emergency management agencies, and better integration of the local police into intelligence briefings would make for stronger security overall. And, as we put together the pieces, we promised that—at any moment—we could scale up security should the intelligence assessments guide us that way. Not only would "drawing down" (that's what we called it) mean greater day-in-day-out security, but by remaining flexible we knew the National Guard could return if needed. We would pivot, if necessary. We assured them we practiced grip.

So we turned the effort into a bit of a political campaign. Lay out the reasons, make the case. We held public meetings and extensive briefings. I asked the National Guard to give a tour of the area, highlighting what could and couldn't be accomplished by their presence. We talked, and explained, and proposed alternatives that would be better for a community that heretofore had looked at this massive complex and thought, Three Mile Island in the era of Al Qaeda.

"You know, people think we're crazy to live here," Judy, a mother of four, told me at one meeting. Her house stood just down the block from the entrance to the plant. "I know so much can happen, so many things can go bad. But it's not like there's anywhere else to go. It's home. This is my home."

She was right. She wasn't staying put because she was oblivious to her surroundings. At some stage, decades before, she had made a calculation about living closer to her parents, near a highway, and in a good public school system. And then things had changed, and she looked out her window and saw a bunch of soldiers. I asked if their presence made her feel safe. "I have four kids," she said. "I wouldn't be doing my job if I thought they were all safe at the same time. I've been worried since the day they were born. Now, it's because two of them have driver's licenses." Judy approached this issue like a security mom. She knew the world was vulnerable, but she tried to make it a little less so for her family. She just wanted to know how.

So we tried to explain it. It took almost a year to get the political, community, and military support for the "drawdown." As I write this, I realize it sounds somewhat absurd to devote so much time and attention to this effort. We're talking about a few guardsmen in a Massachusetts suburb, after all. But we had to do it this way. There was no other template. A slow withdrawal was better than none at all. We began the process as if we were in Afghanistan—we first stopped assigning guardsmen to patrol overnight, then over the weekend, then altogether. We did it with public involvement and full transparency. This represented a new approach to state security.

The residents of Plymouth were ready for that conversation; they understood changes were not only necessary but prudent, even wise. With honest dialogue, they quickly grasped that the National Guard program had been a response to 9/11, and that there were limits to that response. It was a small experiment, but one that would be tested in so many communities as both political and economic realities forced a reassessment of security needs and a revision of entrenched policies.

There is no one-size-fits-all approach to the nation's security. Each city and state will calculate its particular vulnerabilities through localized assessments. Democrats will differ from Republicans in this regard; urban mayors will differ from southern governors. By design, the interplay between local, state, and federal priorities is dynamic—and sometimes very partisan.

In Massachusetts, I kept pushing, aiming for sound policy that was neither too hot nor too cold. I became quite vocal in my criticisms of the Department of Homeland Security. Let me be clear: I was more than vocal. Admittedly, I may have been a little heavy-handed in some of my approaches, but I also saw no other alternative.

In one instance, convinced that federal funds were not being spent efficiently, I took the unusual—and radical—step of stopping all federal funding to local jurisdictions for the purchase of radios and other communications gizmos until the state presented a unified plan for every jurisdiction. Since 9/11, the Department of Homeland Security had distributed billions of dollars to states and urban areas to help them support homeland security efforts. The problem wasn't really the amount of money, but how it was allocated.

The founding fathers anticipated a great many things, but not the logic of government largesse. Because every state has two senators of equal voting power, the state homeland security grant is distributed in a process that is far too democratic. Senators want money for their state, so the standards authorized for distribution tend to favor states equally. This means that while the raw numbers look big for states like New York or Massachusetts, when you actually divide those numbers by the population in each state, the federal government is likely to spend four times as much on an individual citizen in Wyoming as on one in New York or California. As a result, Congress compensated by creating a separate funding source reserved exclusively for cities in order to buttress urban areas, which are more at risk than rural ones.

In Massachusetts, we divided the state into four different homeland security governance areas: west, central, north, and south. (Boston received its own exclusive money pile under the urban program, which reported its expenditures to my office.) Each area has its own committee consisting of members from a broad array of disciplines, from police to firefighters to public health officials. Someone from the state's emergency management agency also sat on each committee to try to integrate the state's efforts with local needs.

When I first started visiting these committees with my deputy Paul, I had every expectation that I would be met with parochial interests and old-school Massachusetts entrenched politics. In some cases I was, but my expectation wasn't entirely accurate. Here were first responders, often working under stressful conditions, who met monthly to vote on security priorities for their communities. They deliberated and debated and came to resolutions that would then be sent to my office for review and authorization. True, the homeland security committees could be demanding, but their inclusive and voluntary nature reflected how democracies should work at their most basic level.

But even in 2007, there was no overarching philosophy to direct these new investments. Money came in from the federal government and then went out to the districts. There was no master plan; from what I could tell, there was barely an outline. It drove me crazy. It had to stop.

"Plans before purchases" became my mantra. I stopped funding. I could find no other way to assess how the state distributed the money that drove so much frenzied purchasing throughout 2007. I was criticized for my heavy-handedness, but we needed a chance to pause. I then spent nine months traveling the state, talking to first responders about their needs and priorities. The final plan may not have been perfect, but it was comprehensive. We set standards for purchases and required each jurisdiction to show how a request was consistent with the state's overall strategy. It forced people to work together—not necessarily because they wanted to, but because they wanted the money.

In those waning years of the Bush administration, states like mine began to assert more independence in the distribution of homeland security funds. They understood, as anyone who watched what happened to New Orleans during Hurricane Katrina would have, that the best use of those funds would be for dual-use and all-hazards planning; a singular focus on terrorism was no longer sustainable. Among states, there was a simple recognition that we had to go back to the kinds of holistic disaster management structures that were promoted by Nixon and the senior Bush when they revamped homeland security efforts during their administrations.

So in late 2007, when DHS released its funding and guidance to states, it was surprising to see how it had revised its grant requirements. DHS told states that 25 percent of all our homeland security funding that year had to be used to counter the potential use of improvised explosive devices (IEDs). It seemed random to demand that jurisdictions as far-ranging as Oklahoma and Oregon all do so, regardless of their specific needs. It came out of nowhere, this attempt to force one-size-fits-all on a homeland that was far from one size. Why not 10 percent? How about 80 percent? I felt someone should challenge the requirement. Indeed, in Massachusetts, we had previously spent more than 25 percent to support agencies in bomb detection and protection efforts, so I felt I could speak out on this DHS policy. The *New York Times* took an interest in the story. They opened an article with a statement I'd made: "Are they serious? IEDs? Like Iraq IEDs?" Homeland Security Secretary Michael Chertoff defended the rule, saying that the federal government had the obligation to set standards for the nation. He was trying to create a unifying vision for the states, just as I was for our own localities. You see the problem? We both had a strong case. But when other states chimed in as well, DHS eventually backed down on the requirement.

Over and over again, what Massachusetts wanted in terms of security was inconsistent with—or, more fairly put, different from— what the Department of Homeland Security advised. Sometimes this tension manifested itself very publicly. DHS's unforgiving stance on immigration issues included a massive federal law enforcement raid in New Bedford, Massachusetts, that affected hundreds of single mothers who were detained as their status was investigated. The governor was not happy with the department, nor with the state agencies that assisted in the roundup. We immediately drove to New Bedford to meet with community members and assure them we would seek amends and release. In one rather pointed phone call, the head of Immigration and Customs Enforcement, an agency that is part of DHS, tried to placate the governor by mentioning that the raid was "perfectly legal." A lawyer as well, Patrick countered: "That seems like a sad safe haven for you."

Many of the changes we enacted required delicacy; no political leader can risk alienating his or her public safety employees. They are often more conservative than not and view new political appointees— liberal, Democratic ones in particular—warily. They can, and often will, just wait us out; I remember hearing a long-term state employee refer to us political appointees as "the Christmas help." One friend of mine who worked in the governor's legal office said that the state police—who still wear a uniform of high black boots and hip-flared pants that look slightly like images from a German World War II movie—represent "a hundred years of tradition, with no progress."

Governor Patrick welcomed progress, even if the Massachusetts State Police sometimes didn't. He was often suspicious of surveillance performed by state police under the rubric of "intelligence sharing," and demanded greater privacy protections over any intelligence shared with the federal government. He had been a civil rights leader, and I had been a civil rights lawyer, and we wanted the state agency he governed to reflect those beliefs, even if the state police didn't seem to mind the status quo. We simply took on some of the worst aspects of an unwieldy and unforgiving system and tried to fix them.

I learned quickly that there is no absolute right answer when it comes to our security. We are forever Goldilocks on a mission. I knew I couldn't make people safe, but I understood I could make them saf*er*. It became clear that the challenge for anyone in charge of security is that acceptable levels of vulnerability are hard to address honestly. Risk is hard to talk about, hard to quantify, and hard not to make personal. As an expert, I can tick off all the risk calculations that go into security planning—I'm more likely to die in a bathtub than from terrorism, for instance—from memory. I can recite facts and probabilities about various risk scenarios. I can scream from the mountaintops that, in the history of mankind, we are statistically safer today than ever before.

But as a mother, I also know that debates about risk center around the value of a human being, and that human being could be my child. And when it comes to each of us individually, and so many of us as parents, there are no expendable children, no acceptable losses. Any risk, even if it's .00001 percent, is too great. You can read to me all the statistics you want, but what if that .00001 percent is actually my child? However unlikely, the risk would be catastrophic if it were Cecilia, Leo, or Jeremiah who was hurt.

In risk theory, this concept of an unlikely, random, and yet consequential event is known as the "black swan." Yes, she exists, and she is so rare that her very appearance will be disruptive to our system. The term was first popularized by Nassim Nicholas Taleb in his book of the same title. We expect to see white swans; they are statistically significant. Black swans are still out there, though, and they represent an utterly random variable whose appearance cannot be predicted by any mathematical calculation or risk assessment. Black swan events represent a complete and extreme outlier, but their existence will alter our equilibrium and possibly change the course of history; 9/11, of course, is the most notorious modern example.

Isn't that what we all fear, that damned black swan? As incredibly unlikely as she is, I can't simply write her off, because I, too, have no expendable children. I can repeat every statistical analysis I know about the likelihood of a crisis, and still I've got that black swan in the back of my head, that random happening that might take one of them away from me.

It might be some solace to remember that we constantly play the odds every day. As parents, we fight against our instinct to lock the doors and keep our children home forever. Yes, we want them to be safe at all times, but we also want them to learn to ride a bike, do cartwheels, have sleepovers, go to overnight camp, eventually get a driver's license, and then, in a blink, venture forth on their own. So we do everything we can to minimize the risk, knowing that we can keep our children *safer* but that we can't promise they will be *perfectly* safe. We don't think of it that way, but as parents we make millions of judgments that allow them to grow while still prioritizing their safety. We are always calibrating some notion of acceptable loss.

This is true in the home, and it should be true in the homeland as well. To some extent, we do this already. We don't tolerate more rigorous screening on city subways because that would hinder our capacity to go to and from work: We have decided that the benefits of smooth travel outweigh the risk of some potential loss. We don't stop every cargo ship coming in from some foreign land; if we did, the Amazon.com orders of holiday gifts wouldn't arrive on time. Each of these decisions is a subtle form of acceptable loss planning, just like any military general would perform to determine the way forward in battle. And recognizing that we have already made these choices may help us understand why our nation isn't as safe as it might be. We can't build a society simply to prevent the black swan from appearing.

If we could talk honestly about how we have affirmatively chosen to be unsafe, some of the struggles surrounding our homeland security could be solved. We could start to make better calibrations about risk and consequence, freeing us from a system that is too often tied to the last threat, too often stuck in the past.

I sometimes worry that the body American was—and maybe still is—suffering from PTSD. We overreact too easily, so that any stimulus becomes a perceived threat without discernment. That's why money poured into cities and states as potential risks were used to justify buying new fire trucks and new police radios, building new emergency operations centers, or (in the most famous case of homeland security funding going awry) new air conditioner systems for trash trucks. More, more, more.

This philosophy—more than any single policy or program—is what I hoped to change when I agreed to serve as Governor Patrick's homeland security advisor.

We have to train the body to recalibrate. We will face risks, but not all of them require action, let alone overreaction. For one thing, if we just throw money at every potential threat, it simply means that we've spent a lot of money—and not necessarily devised a strategy. As the state's homeland security advisor, I heard countless pleas from police departments that began with an invocation of 9/11. And again and again, I heard hints that any limit on their spending amounted to letting the terrorists win—as if questioning a police department's need for new radios somehow would lead to the next 9/11.

State government allowed me enough flexibility to slowly dismantle—essentially, cool off—safety and security efforts. I believed that the state needed to move toward resiliency, toward an acceptance that at some stage we have to accept saf*er* as the smarter standard. If "too hot" is the only route, then we are all eventually headed to the bunkers, literally. We need to let go a little, skin a few knees, and accept that the black swan is out there.

What Massachusetts accomplished with the National Guard and the Pilgrim facility was, admittedly, a small piece of a huge apparatus. But for other states that were watching, there was something liberating in what we did. Many states in the homeland also needed to be freed from policies and procedures they'd inherited post-9/11. This small adventure in security drawdown provided a road map for how they might begin to alter their security apparatuses, one program at a time, when the conditions called for it. Once Massachusetts announced its change, every other state that still had National Guard members at its nuclear facilities followed our lead.

Security is somewhat elusive—sometimes way too hot and sometimes way too cold—but we can keep searching for just right. We must change as circumstances change, and the measures we enact to keep us safer may be satisfactory only for a little while, but that may be just long enough. Nothing remains the same: it's a basic fact. A resilient society anticipates it.

And, as I would soon learn, so does a resilient family.

HOPE FLOATS

DAVID AND I ADAPTED, OR PERHAPS FELL, INTO A NEW ROUTINE THAT WORKED for us. David had secured tenure, I was advising the governor on issues I loved, and the kids thrived at school. Times were busy and we could have used more date nights, but we were exceptionally happy.

I remember at one deployment ceremony for the National Guard, when our state troops were still being sent to Afghanistan, I sat next to a mother preparing for a yearlong tour of duty. She had three young children. I asked her how she was planning on managing her home life. She looked at me as if she couldn't believe the question: "I don't manage, Secretary Kayyem. I deal." I suspected, in our less extreme way, that David and I had learned to deal.

Then, in late October 2008, while we were sitting in the movie theater with the kids watching *High School Musical 3*, David and I received near simultaneous phone calls. The buzzing interrupted the graduation mix of "We're All In This Together."

In preparation for a possible victory in November 2008, Obama's advisors asked experts and supporters from across the country to stop what they were doing, move to DC, and assist the Democratic nominee. These volunteers would spend hours at designated agencies or departments, reviewing policies and budget priorities to prepare for a potential change of leadership. An agency review team (ART) of about twelve to sixteen experts was created for each department. Each ART met with George W. Bush's top leadership, diving into the depths of governmental bureaucracy and emerging to report back to Obama's campaign. Each ART produced a twenty-five-page document; all together, the report could have been entitled "Damn, This Government Is Big." It prioritized the major issues that Obama would confront should he make it to day one. Republican contender John McCain had the same setup.

The calls were quite unexpected, especially because we had supported Hillary Clinton early in the primary. David was contacted by the Justice Department team; I heard from the Department of Homeland Security team. The process began with a few conference calls, but should Obama win, we would be expected to volunteer our time (not to mention our frequent-flier miles) and work our butts off in DC. We agreed. And then Obama won. So many years later, it is sometimes hard to imagine the sense of excitement his election ignited, both here and abroad. He is an exceptional president, a person who takes the long view. Regardless of my early support for Clinton, I was on the bandwagon now.

I knew some of Obama's homeland security policy advisors, such as Rand Beers, Randy Beardsworth, and Clark Kent Ervin. Governor Patrick granted me leave, and David cleared out his teaching schedule. My parents flew in from Los Angeles to help us out, and David's parents let us stay at their house in DC, in the bedroom where David grew up. We managed the days away with constant e-mails and calls with the kids. We became expert US Airways Shuttle fliers. We simply dealt.

And so did my parents. When we told them that the Obama campaign had called both of us, they didn't even wait for us to ask. Luckily, my father's work in Los Angeles affords him considerable flexibility, and my mother spends about half her time on the East Coast visiting my sister and me anyway. I still wonder how these warm weather–loving parents of mine managed to send three kids to school or pre-school every day of that cold winter. As ever, they didn't flinch when we asked them to carry this tremendous weight; they were calm in the midst of a seismic shift for our family. We left our kids—and our dirty dishes—to them, with long lists of instructions and lots of phone numbers. My mother said to me, "I'm too old to go work in government, but these are exciting times, so you two go do it for us."

I had never visited DHS in its NAC headquarters before the day I arrived to critique it. The majority of Obama's DHS transition team lived in DC, and many of them had working relationships with the Bush administration. I wasn't one of them. When the taxi dropped me off that first day, I kept wondering where I was supposed to go; the complex resembled a fenced-in retirement campus dotted with bland two-story buildings. My mother-in-law, who passed by the

NAC every single day, remarked she never knew that the department was there. In plain sight, so as to seem innocuous. This was, in part, by design.

I came prepared to work, and work hard. Attacks often occur during, or close to, transitions from one government to another. The USS *Cole* attack was at the end of Clinton's term, and the post-9/11 attacks in Madrid and London happened immediately before or after their elections. New people and new policies create vulnerabilities. If our enemies thought about it, they would have realized that this particular transition had unique vulnerabilities.

Obama would be the first new president to take office after 9/11. And Obama wasn't just any president. His background and race had already generated enough hatred to make him the most protected candidate in the history of the United States government. Now he was president-elect, and with his two young children, the Secret Service—a component within DHS—was on the highest of alerts.

What's more, this would be the first transition for DHS, and the first group of Democrats to take charge of the department, which was formed under Republican leadership. Unlike at the Justice or State Departments, where long lines of "formers" are called upon for assistance, we had no one. Tom Ridge and Michael Chertoff, both Republicans, were the only former heads around. No political appointee from the Democratic Party had ever governed at DHS.

This meant that the transition team faced a considerable learning curve. We focused on the basics: We needed to figure out how the department worked. We sat in a secure conference room and listened to various reports from the trenches. Camped out in an empty second-floor annex, twentysomething volunteers from the Obama campaign helped us put together the pieces of a staggering number of briefings. There was considerable talent on both sides of the table. Given my role in Massachusetts, I brought a new perspective to the discussions, drawing on my knowledge of the relationship between DHS and the states.

Secretary Chertoff couldn't have been kinder to such an ideologically different group. He never once suggested that he held ill will toward me for my more public protests of DHS, including the *New York Times* article on the 25 percent rule. He made his staff available to us. He must have spent between thirty and forty hours in briefings. Indeed, he seemed to relish that we were now in the cradle of so-called incompetency. This long-distance runner who is wicked smart said to me coyly, "Now you'll see it's much harder than it seems."

The transition meetings continued up until the inauguration. In those frenzied weeks, David and I never explicitly discussed the long-term consequences of this commitment. We had chosen our careers and we could pretend that it would be exciting for the kids to move to DC, that it would teach them how to be resilient, and all of the things us parents tell ourselves to make ourselves feel better. We decided, but we didn't focus on the details: If David and I both took jobs with the new administration, the kids would have to transition, too. If one of us got a job, then that parent would travel back and forth and we would be a commuter family. There were no parenting books devoted to how to manage this potential dilemma. We knew families who were planning for the same uncertain future; one parent would travel, but the kids would stay put. For us, that made a lot of sense. If

I didn't get a job in the administration, I didn't want to move to DC unnecessarily, especially if that meant we couldn't keep the kids in the schools they loved.

After seven weeks of furious work, many who had served on the transition teams accepted positions in the new administration and immediately found themselves working in the departments they had once scrutinized. David had been approached to rejoin the Justice Department as deputy assistant attorney general at the Office of Legal Counsel, an office that had become infamous during the Bush years for authoring the "torture memos." (David was slated to run that office until the nominee for assistant attorney general was confirmed; she never was, so David was "acting" head for his entire two-year tenure.)

I did not receive an offer.

In early January, the transition teams disbanded and new cabinet secretaries were chosen. These secretaries, in turn, began to form their own teams. Former Arizona governor Janet Napolitano had been picked to run DHS, but I didn't know her at all and I couldn't predict whether she would ask me to join the department. The White House appointment process was anything but transparent, and while I thought it was likely that I would be offered a job, it wasn't clear where or when or what. I just had to wait.

We traveled with the whole family to DC to witness the inauguration, which would prove to be a historic event. Two days before the ceremony, I interviewed with Napolitano in a building that housed the transition teams. The bare office was staffed with her colleagues from Arizona. We talked about what position I wanted, and I mentioned the two that interested me the most: assistant secretary for intergovernmental affairs and assistant secretary for policy. We had a good rapport. I even advised her on her lipstick choice for a *Vanity Fair* layout the new cabinet was going to do later that day. And then I left. For all I knew, I might have forever been known as the woman who bombed her interview with Napolitano because she told her red was better than pink.

David started working on the very first hour of the very first day of the new administration. On Inauguration Day, January 20, 2009, he finalized documents that would be the first that Obama signed as president. On January 21, as David awoke to the first of many early-morning phone calls from the White House counsel, I packed the car and drove the kids the eight hours home to Cambridge. It was a cold and miserable trip. It finally struck me that, in fact, this could become routine: We would visit a father and husband who no longer lived with us. Contemplating my professional disappointment and our indefinite family separation, I blasted Rascal Flatts (soothing for me, annoying for the kids) the whole way home.

The next few weeks were dreadfully long. Had I blown the interview? Day after day, there was no call from DHS. David was in DC running one of the most powerful legal offices in the country, and I was dealing with Steve, the tile guy. There had been a cold spell during that Christmas break and our laundry-room pipes had burst, destroying the entire dining room below. I had to deal with insurance and contractors and workers and Steve coming in to assess and fix the damage all by myself. I wasn't very nice to David, who was often getting to his parents' house after midnight, eating a plate of leftovers prepared by his mother, and falling asleep in his childhood bedroom. He missed the kids. I was bitter about our living situation. My dear friends Tory and Allie often came over late at night with wine and plastic glasses (due to the construction, the only way to access my kitchen was by going outside through the back patio, and it was too cold to bother) to help me pass the time.

The kids certainly knew something could be up. Cecilia kept saying, "I know we're moving." Sometimes, she said it as if it were a statement. Other times, she asked it as if it were a question. I couldn't answer honestly—or even admit I'd had the interview, because I didn't want her to be as anxious as I was.

I resumed my duties at the statehouse. Then, on Tuesday in the first week of March, my cell phone rang unexpectedly as I drove home. I turned the corner onto my street and pulled over. It was not Napolitano but Brian, one of her senior aides. He offered me the position of assistant secretary for intergovernmental affairs. This person would act as the point of contact in the department for the fifty states and hundreds of cities, territories, and tribal areas. In effect, I was being asked to answer the phone that I had once called from Massachusetts to discuss and debate government policy on funding, and, in the event of a crisis, operational response. Chertoff's comment—*this is much harder than it seems*—was long forgotten.

"Yes," I said stupidly. I had no bargaining chips after that.

"Great, I'll get you on the phone with the secretary this week," Brian said. "Can you be here in two weeks?"

You've got to be kidding me, I thought. "Yes," I said stupidly, again. "We have three kids but a lot of help, and we'll deal."

I had at least done some homework. Over the previous few weeks, still hoping that I would get a job with the administration, I had sought advice about the best ways to introduce the kids to the idea of the move. I spoke with my friends in the military and with my colleagues in the National Guard, those women who knew how to "deal." They move their families quite regularly, in times of war and peace, and readily shared their secrets. Counterintuitively, they had learned that, if possible, young kids should end a school year in the new location. Moving during the summer would mean spending hot months in a new home, without friends, just waiting and worrying about the first day of school. This way, the kids could join sports teams, get to know classmates, and feel more confident as September approached. I convinced myself everything would be fine, using the language of my profession: We would minimize their risk of a long summer of isolation and prepare them for the years ahead. We had a plan.

I quietly began to say goodbye to our Massachusetts life as we knew it. David and I agreed that we'd break the news to the kids when he returned to Cambridge. I traveled to DC—without telling the kids—to find a rental house and to enroll them in a public school where they already had friends. I resigned from my position at the statehouse and said goodbye to the governor. I secured backup baby-sitting in DC for Jeremiah, since we couldn't get him into preschool immediately. I re-registered the cars, filled out change-of-address forms, and put our house in Cambridge up for rent.

That was the easy part. David returned home one weekend, and we strategized on the best way to tell the kids.

I planned on taking a cue from the Obama campaign poster. If we contextualized the move for the older kids in terms of the "hope" of the new administration, I thought they might grasp the sense of civic duty we felt. We sat them down in the den. I mentally ran through my rousing call to arms. And then David stated, plainly: "Your mother also got a job in DC, and we will all be moving down in two weeks." The boys greeted the news silently; Jeremiah barely understood. They learned that our new place would be just a few blocks from where David's parents lived, and that my parents were going to help with the move by taking them to Disney World while we packed up the house. None of these bells and whistles changed the fact that we were leaving before the end of the school year.

Cecilia, at seven years old, protested the most, feeling that such a monumental decision shouldn't just be delivered to her all wrapped up in a bow.

"No one else can do your jobs?" she asked. "You're the *only* ones who can do them?"

It was a great question, and the answer was no. We weren't essential, and we knew that. Goodness, I had spent much of my career talking about creating redundancies, making sure that no single part of the system was truly indispensable. So of course, as Cecilia noted, this was all optional. There were promises we could make—the White House Easter egg hunt; a family picture with the president—but we also knew the kids would make sacrifices, too.

David didn't make it back again to Cambridge, so I moved the house on my own. We hadn't found renters and wouldn't for a few months; again, our timing was off, and there were no takers until the summer. I had to pack, organize, and get whatever we wanted down to

DC by truck. I found some cheap movers, but as we loaded the rental, it became clear that we would need more space. I rushed to a U-Haul. With no one else available, I drove the unwieldy second rental eight hours to DC. I arrived at two a.m., parked it at a local gas station near my in-laws', and paid the attendant forty bucks to watch it until morning, when I could get into the new house. Despite the hour, David was at work, a brutal hint at what our new life would be like.

As I stood, filthy and middle-of-the-night exhausted, under the harsh lights emanating from some seedy gas station, I couldn't help but feel excited. I was days away from starting a great job as a political appointee in an administration that everyone was dying to join. It was my introduction to the old truism that exercises in hope often entail a fair amount of sleep deprivation—as a mother of three, you'd have thought I had learned.

I can say now that the boys, then five and three, transitioned well enough. Cecilia never adapted to the city, and she would hate me for saying anything more, so I'll leave it at that. (She's also a teenager now, so I fear the consequences of getting on her bad side.) Leo attended a public school near the house and was thrilled by its sports program. That was all we ever heard, and that was good enough. We lived at the DC and Maryland border, so the neighborhood had an urban feel with suburban perks. Unlike at our city home in Cambridge, Leo could walk to a friend's house and ride his bike to his after-school activities. It was an amazing freedom for a second grader.

Jeremiah eventually was accepted into a part-time nursery program and spent his mornings there. Cara, one of our beloved babysitters from Boston, was looking for a change of scene and came down to Washington with us, providing some welcomed consistency. Jeremiah's day care was spectacularly precious—its only flaw was that it assumed a level of commitment from parents that we could never satisfy. By my third child, I was tired of trying so hard. To this day I don't know if he was my easiest toddler because of his disposition or because I didn't notice otherwise.

Once I was in DC, I had to give up on the idea of mastering all the details of the kids' lives. It was no longer possible. So I created many backups and redundancies in the system: Cara moved down with us from Cambridge, my in-laws were just a few miles away, a long list of additional babysitters was ready to help, and my parents visited often enough. I found it hard to let go, until I realized that I couldn't just be half-in. I couldn't manage a playdate with other parents by e-mail in the morning and then be unreachable for the rest of the day because I was in a classified briefing, where no cell phones are allowed. It was unfair to everyone, most of all the kids. I slowly but eventually completely began to let others take care of the details.

It wasn't possible any other way. From my first day on the job, I attended a daily early-morning meeting with other senior leadership, sometimes with the secretary herself, to map out issues that might arise over the next twenty-four hours. I traveled often, as one of the obligations of my job was to visit the "homeland" of my title. While I had some capacity to control the late-night meetings, and a young and talented staff—Jarrod, Stephanie, Amanda, Drew, Fayrouz, Matt, Alaina, Kellyn, and Jon—who could cover for me, I was too often on a BlackBerry during my hours away from the office. I wasn't paying a lot of attention to the home.

So I was surprised when, soon after our move, I received an e-mail from the preschool requesting a meeting. I figured Jeremiah's stubbornness, those eyelashes and curls notwithstanding, had finally pushed them too far. But I wasn't even close. His teachers had noticed that his capacity to identify colors was inadequate. We had noticed the same, and it was a sort of running joke in the family that Jeremiah was going to grow up to be goth.

I was escorted into the director's room, where I took a seat across from three middle-aged women wearing Birkenstocks and worried expressions. "We want you to know that there is nothing wrong with Jeremiah. We just believe," the head nurse said, "that he may be color-blind." She then began a meandering discourse about the genetic ailment and ways we could teach him to counteract it, and even offered up names of some famous people who were also color-blind.

Jeremiah, for some time, had been drawing in grays and blacks only. I had feared that all the changes—the move, his parents' absences—were leaving deep psychological scars. But color-blindness—it was such an obvious explanation that I was embarrassed I hadn't thought of it. My father is color-blind, and his preferred hues trend toward gray and black as well. The recessive gene passes through daughters to their sons, so it made sense that I would be a carrier.

This explanation was only a partial consolation. I still felt horrible. I had failed to identify this phenomenon, despite noticing it months before. What kind of mother can't figure this out on her own? How had I so obviously missed the details of my child's life? Hey, idiot, I thought, your kid is drawing in blacks and grays, picks the same colors in clothes, your own father is color-blind, it's a genetic mutation passed on through the maternal DNA, and you didn't put it together until three women who see your kid for a few hours each morning sat you down and told you? I was caught up in all the details of my new job, managing the drama and momentous changes at home, caught up in the novelty of everything. I sheepishly explained the diagnosis to Jeremiah. I told him I could be around more to help him learn to adapt. He went upstairs to compare the colors he was seeing with Leo's answers. He thought it was cool. And, thankfully, he didn't take me up on my offer to be home more. Maybe he already knew it was a promise I couldn't guarantee.

My work was just too overwhelming. The biggest challenge for the new team coming into DHS was the same one I confronted in state government: when anything can go wrong, and you're charged with making sure nothing does, how can you effectively pivot, amend, ratchet down, alter, and change priorities? During the transition, we had heard from the Bush team about the various DHS programs and policies that they felt were most important. Chertoff had a sense of what he wanted to pass on to the new team, and, again, he was gracious with his time. But as the transition team listened to the challenges facing an agency none of us had ever worked in before, it was a little debilitating to hear just how *essential* every program was to America's security. Various directors or component heads would come in, explain that they administered the *one* program that was keeping the whole sorry mess of American security together, and warn that there would be considerable and unknowable risks if we were to disband it. Who were we to question them?

As we made our own assessments of how to prioritize Obama's homeland security strategy, we were left with a lingering feeling of paralysis: What if they were right? The changes that we hoped to implement carried risks. As I mentioned, transitions, historically, have been times when terrorists carry out their attacks. As if to highlight this point in the starkest terms, Michael Chertoff remained as secretary until one day into Obama's presidency. He stepped down on January 21, 2007. It was a voluntary agreement to ensure that the agency was as stable as possible on the very day it might be needed the most.

But as we, the new secretary's senior staff, settled into our roles, we looked for ways to define the new administration and the new DHS. Our first target couldn't have been plainer: It was like a neon flashing light—or, more specifically, it was green-yellow-orange-red.

Early on, the White House convened a meeting to discuss the status of the infamous color-code system. It was well understood by then that the system was unworkable and even subject to abuse; the public could not understand what they were supposed to do when the alert color changed—exactly when do we break out the duct tape, and what, precisely, do we do with it?

First created in March 2002, the color-code system was meant to provide a "comprehensive and effective means to disseminate information regarding the risk of terrorist acts to federal, state, and local authorities and to the American people." The problem was that no transparent and objective criteria existed by which the public could understand when and why the alert system would change. Therefore, it was subject to manipulation. Tom Ridge, who oversaw the implementation of the system, even wrote in *The Test of Our Times* that he was pressured by then defense secretary Donald Rumsfeld to raise the alert level on the eve of the November 2004 presidential election based on a bin Laden video that had just been released. Ridge pushed back, but wrote, "After that episode, I knew I had to follow through with my plans to leave the federal government for the private sector." The ease with which the existing system could be co-opted for purposes other than national safety was obvious. In the absence of clear criteria and controls, the possibility of someone changing the nation's alert stance on no more evidence than "just because" was too great.

When the Obama administration came in, it was all but pre-ordained that the existing alert system would end. That we had the blessing of former DHS heads Michael Chertoff and Tom Ridge didn't hurt. But change is slow, sometimes.

Two very long years later, we finally replaced the colors with a system called the National Terrorism Advisory System. The delay was akin to the difficulties that I had experienced in Plymouth; cooling down is complicated. The problem with dismantling the color-code system was that, over the years it was in place, it had so infiltrated the entire homeland's security apparatus that simply turning it off was impossible. Expectations, again, had formed. Cities and states had aligned their own security-apparatus planning to changes in the color code. Funding mechanisms to first responders were often driven by the level of threat. Various federal agencies—including the Coast Guard and the Transportation Security Administration—had detailed protocols in place for any adjustment to the threat status triggered by a shift in color. Each had to be identified, addressed, dismantled, and reassembled so that a new system—one that used common

English as a form of communication and that had identifiable criteria built in—could take its place. It took that long to defeat a universally reviled villain.

There was also one clever aspect to the new policy: We ensured that no one else would have to go through what we were going through just then. The National Terrorism Advisory System has a built in drawdown. Any change to an elevated threat level can be in place for only two weeks, maximum. After that, this or future administrations would have to justify continuing the heightened alert every two weeks. We purposefully built an all clear into the system.

The color-code dilemma, along with a couple dozen others, would fill those early days at DHS. There was no immediate crisis except an economic one; the White House's focus was on saving us from the proverbial fiscal cliff. I used the time to get briefed on terror threats, intelligence gaps, state and local planning, earthquake fears, hurricane season, droughts, fires, illegal border crossings, the drug trade off our coasts, potential cyberattacks, increased intelligence chatter against the president, and failing crucial infrastructure. I was on the road eight to ten days a month, so we scheduled our lives accordingly. Quickly, the kids fell into a routine at their new schools, playing after-school games and hanging out in the neighborhood. This was too good to be true. Everything was working. At last, after so many months preparing the transfer of responsibility from political appointee to political appointee, after the stress and physical exhaustion of the move, after the change-of-address forms were complete, with the rental house feeling like ours, I was ready for anything.

Hope!

GET IN LINE LIKE EVERYBODY ELSE

DAMN HOPE.

Just a few weeks after my arrival at DHS, a young official from the department's intelligence office called me. They wanted me to attend a briefing in their secure building in the NAC. I wasn't told what it was about, but I also didn't sense that this was an immediate emergency. I walked casually toward the meeting only to learn that it had switched locales; it was to be held in the secretary's suite of offices. Now I was a bit more alarmed, but for more mundane reasons. I found myself running across the campus, not wanting to be late to an official meeting with Napolitano.

Her offices were designed as a SCIF (pronounced "skiff"), short for Sensitive Compartmented Information Facility, so that classified conversations could occur in the open without any fears of surveillance or foreign spying. The secretary's office is also highly fortified. Even if someone could sneak through the massive security apparatus that guards all entries to DHS, they would have to pass a few more guards and a steel door to even reach the hallway that contains another steel door that, eventually, leads to the secretary's offices. Holding out my badge before me, I was waved through each layer of defense.

A young man sat next to the secretary, ready to brief her senior staff. These "briefers" exist throughout government: They are not authorized to give commentary or answer value-laden questions. They simply present the known facts, and often that means just re-telling information that another agency has in its possession.

He calmly explained that a new virus had been diagnosed in Veracruz, Mexico, and that it had likely lingered there for some time before it was officially identified. Furthermore, it was a fast killer, and it was spreading quickly throughout Mexico. There was no way to prevent the virus from crossing the border—in all likelihood, it was already here. There was no known vaccine. The Mexican government was deliberating on how best to close public and private facilities, a process known as "social distancing." Because this virus spread from person to person and not through food, the most aggressive tactic was to create very few opportunities for people to get together; this meant shuttering schools, public meetings, sporting events. The World Health Organization (WHO) was holding executive committee meetings to determine whether they would elevate the virus to pandemic status.

Just like that, I had been introduced to H1N1. We thought we had prepared for all contingencies, but H1N1 wasn't in the briefing books.

Napolitano brought us all into her conference room. "When will we hear from the WHO?" she said to her chief of staff. "And what happens when they tell us we're all going to die?" She smiled. It was her way of calming everyone. Napolitano is one of the funniest people I have ever met. She is tough, no question, and yelled when work was unsatisfactory or comments were unclear. Never once did I think she was being unfair, only insistent. If I screwed up, she would simply let me know it. She and I became friendly early on; there were so few women at the department that the female political appointees formed a close unit. We would go for drinks and bitch about this or that. I often clashed with her transplanted staff from Arizona, a group that a number of DHS employees called the "cactus cabal." But Napolitano was always accessible—sometimes too much so. Once, she was so bored during a major storm covering the DC area and mid-Atlantic states that she proceeded to call all the governors and mayors from North Carolina to Connecticut just to make sure, she told me, "that everything is okay." She just liked people and knew how to keep her team loyal. After one long spell of intense work, she gave me a gift certificate for a fancy massage. How could I not be loyal? At that first meeting on H1N1, she exhibited a command of details and a curiosity about the road ahead.

The secretary's chief medical advisor went on to explain the numbers. There was little good news: The last swine flu pandemic involving the H1N1 influenza virus was in 1918, and it had killed up to 5 percent of the world's population. The 2009 virus, however, was a new and unique strain of H1N1. It was a strange assortment of bird and human flu viruses combined with a Eurasian pig flu virus—hence "swine" flu. But what made it highly unusual and scary was that, unlike most flu outbreaks, H1N1 did *not* disproportionately infect adults older than sixty years of age. Influenza kills several Americans every year, overwhelmingly the very old and very young, or people whose immune systems are already compromised. H1N1, it seemed, could bring down the healthiest among us.

Pandemic planning was established long before H1N1 was first identified in Mexico. The Department of Health and Human Services (HHS), the Centers for Disease Control (CDC), DHS, and state and local officials had spent years learning the lessons of the anthrax response and attempting to merge the culturally disparate disciplines of public health and public safety. They are two very different fields, and the personalities of the professionals who are drawn toward each couldn't be more distinct. Public health officials tend to be community oriented, inclusive, and egalitarian; public safety officials, particularly when confronting a crisis, tend to be more militaristic, hierarchical, and demanding.

All of America's pandemic planning had been based on recent cases, not the 1918 flu. That meant that there were all sorts of protocols for a potential outbreak of something that starts really far away: SARS hit Asia in 2002, and the avian (H5N1) virus started in China in 2005. Then, the government had focused on limiting transportation and border travel, with considerable reaction time to make our plans. We'd insufficiently considered the possibility that a virus could originate in North America. The simple truth was H1N1 was basically already here. There was no time to plan. We had to act.

That small briefing in the secretary's office became a mobilization to confront a global threat at a sprinter's pace. Within the first two weeks of its identification, the WHO and the CDC had to simply stop counting cases of H1N1. Europeans, somehow immune from North America's worries, recommended residents cancel all inessential travel to the continent. Facing a threat they couldn't see, the world decided the threat was the Americas and, indeed, Americans. Compounding the sense of isolation, several countries established travel quarantines against *visitors* from North America. We were left alone to fend off this new menace.

The flu had quickly turned into a global pandemic, a word that has some technical, scientific meaning that describes the strength of the virus and its ease of transmission. In English, the translation is something like "Oh sh-t."

Nothing about the federal response was going to be easy. There was no vaccine readily available; without it, all of our efforts, including social distancing, were mere stopgaps against the virus's spread. And once a vaccine was identified and manufactured, a massive production and distribution system had to be set up. Preparations for the 2004 and 2005 avian flu outbreaks helped. When that flu started in Asia, it killed nearly 50 percent of those infected, and it left a legacy of planning by public health entities. But because public health threats did not get the same amount of attention as other homeland security threats, our response to H1N1 would depend on an underserved health care system.

The only good news was that this flu was identified in the spring, when the hard-core flu season was still several months away. So the administration spent those months buttressing public health efforts, educating first responders, and waiting. Every season, massive flu-vaccination programs are put into place; a second influenza program was simply put on top of the normal seasonal plan, assuming a vaccine to H1N1 could be identified and mass-produced. President Obama declared H1N1 a national emergency and vested Secretary of Health and Human Services Kathleen Sebelius with the authority to grant waivers to hasten vaccine testing, expedite vaccine production, and let loose the resources that would be needed to deliver them.

My department is about command and control; that is why the Homeland Security Presidential Directive (HSPD-5), which governs the roles and responsibilities in a crisis, was written into law. Because this was a government response to the unfolding crisis, DHS was responsible for working with the fifty governors and their emergency management and public safety teams to distribute the vaccine. The vaccination program was about logistics and communication; this wasn't merely a public health issue. In addition, we are the border enforcement agency and had to protect our personnel working there. If H1N1 wasn't already in the United States, it was coming across soon.

Immediately after I first learned of H1N1, my office instituted a regular call to all fifty state governors and their public safety teams to provide information that they could communicate to their constituencies. Governors, police officers, emergency managers, even members of the state National Guards all had reasonable concerns about how the virus, and the vaccine process, would spread.

During those calls, I would relate the pace of vaccine production and the challenges of distribution and, just as important, why those challenges existed. I was always honest about what we knew and what we didn't know. The information conveyed was basic, often simplified to the most accessible details. Medical experts, like the head of the CDC, were also available to answer technical questions. Napolitano would join in; as a former governor, she loved talking to her peers.

We weren't just making phone calls to be nice. Accurate information is crucial in any crisis. But it also provides an opportunity for those who are looked to for leadership to learn details that they don't receive because they are too often handed a series of talking points. It is the details that are both educational and reassuring; nothing is more humiliating to a public official than not knowing the answer to a constituent's desperate question about protecting his children. Those twice-a-week calls were honest and sometimes frustrating, but always educational.

In one of those early calls, the governors were instructed about plans to identify, manufacture, and distribute a vaccine. Without question, political leaders, public health and safety officials, and first responders would receive the vaccine first to ensure their own strength so they could continue to help others. One governor asked if first families were considered part of the political leadership team. That answer, I told him, was up to each governor. Only they could best address the equities of vaccinating their own children.

It was a fair question. I had the same one, too. What about my kids?

H1N1 was a child's disease; it was first identified in two children. Neither had been in contact with pigs. The first confirmed H1N1 pandemic flu death in the United States was of a toddler from Mexico City who was visiting family in Brownsville, Texas.

This disaster quickly became personal. Every day I'd hear the worst-case scenarios, because that is what we have to envision, from the potential death toll to the disastrous economic impact as workers—sick, afraid, or both—stay home. All I saw were the bad consequences. That was the job description.

Unlike some faraway international crisis, every aspect of this response, as it unfolded over those few months, needed to focus on the home. Since personal conduct was the key to reducing transmission, almost immediately we tried to re-educate the American public on, of all things, how to sneeze correctly. Cover your nose and mouth with your elbow, not your hand. Honestly, who knew? As we tried to master the "bend of your elbow" stance, we were informed that the reasoning behind it was that the elbow area is wider than most palms and tends not to be used for other purposes. Makes sense. I was sold. But now we were responsible for getting America to cough and sneeze in this new way. It had to become the norm. So we quickly reviewed documents that would be sent out nationwide to teach people to defy their instincts and, quite possibly, the training of their mothers and grandmothers.

The kids came back from school one day with those nifty handouts showing a cool stick figure doing the elbow cough. The kids tested it, thought it "worked" (whatever that meant), and scolded David and me for failing to follow their lead. I was somewhat comforted by their admonitions; it meant that our decisions had had some impact.

But a new way to sneeze only gets you so far. My days were book-ended by early-morning calls covering details of the H1N1 threat and returning home to monitor my kids' health, and all I knew was: They needed that vaccine. A vaccination would be proof positive that I'd done something to ward off an invisible threat.

Once identified, the delivery of the vaccine would go to designated public health facilities depending on need, capacity, and population. Those deliveries would be secure and protected, and then a long and intricate process of distribution to local public health facilities, community centers, private doctors, and schools would occur. The simple rules we had devised were that first responders and public health officials would get it first; then each state would decide how to prioritize and administer the rest. We had to leave it to the states, with guidance from the federal government, because the states understood how best to manage their own public health apparatus.

Simply put, it meant that in DC, my kids would have to stand in line just like everyone else. Viewed from within the department, it was a thing of logical beauty. Viewed from my kitchen, it sucked.

And I wasn't alone in thinking that there was a way to game it all. I noticed—and quickly—that most requests related to my status in government came from friends or family. They asked for a White House tour, or they wondered if there was extra space at the Easter Egg hunt. Answers: it depends and no. My professional expertise was of less interest to them, until H1N1.

That Jen, my old college friend, was the first call didn't surprise me. She had a newborn, some health issues, and two older girls, and needed help. Then my sister called. She wondered if I knew anyone in New York City who had a stash. Later I got texts from two more friends, both mothers.

Even a colleague who worked on immigration issues at the White House pulled me aside one day at the Eisenhower Executive Office Building. "Isn't there any extra?" she asked, showing me pictures of her two children. Everyone tried to skip in line. The desperate phone calls seem absurd in hindsight. Again and again I was asked: "Can you get me the vaccine?" It felt like a drug deal, sordid and secret. Except I didn't have the answer they wanted.

There are no perks to being a disaster management expert. I know, as I've been doing it for some time. Sure, there are fancy helicopter rides and car services and (don't tell anyone) a space in the Boston Marathon reserved for runners who are public safety officials. But a general truth about holding a job in security or safety is that you are usually getting yelled at or yelling at someone. I know that sounds harsh, and it isn't meant to suggest that the people I worked with weren't (mostly) amazing and committed government employees. It's just that when you are preparing for the worst, the pace is relentless.

As DHS's assistant secretary for intergovernmental affairs, I would be given an early dose of the vaccine. I was enjoined, however, from assisting my own kids. They had to wait. There simply wasn't enough. I was as desperate and angry as every other parent, even though I knew the reasons why the vaccine was administered this way. It wasn't easy being both a public servant, dutifully administering the plan to protect the most children possible, and a mother, whose own kids come before all others.

Even once the manufacturing and production of the vaccine was at full force over the course of that fall, it still needed to be distributed from federal production centers to every public health facility. There were two dramatic and logistical challenges that remained: the first involved deciding on the amount and timing for delivery to each state, and the second involved a state's decision as to how to administer the vaccine to its citizens.

The first challenge amounts to a kind of sibling rivalry. The nature of our federal structure makes it so. The general rule about federalism is that the fifty states are like most families: They have their common enemies, like the federal bureaucracy that hands down regulations. They have their common friends, like the federal bureaucracy that doles out largesse of various sorts and sizes. But underneath it all is a fear that the guy or gal next door is somehow doing better than you, somehow getting a better deal, somehow making you look bad. Like most families, dynamics are often about birth order and special (though not always successful) pleadings.

When a nation in the grip of a pandemic does not have enough vaccine, even while it produces it as fast as it can, when schools are being closed and people are dying and the threat of a really bad thing happening seems more likely than not, who gets to go first matters. It matters a lot. Who goes first: Who gets out first, who gets supplies first, who is the most needy, and who is the most deserving? The corollary to that dynamic is equally unattractive: Why the hell did they get out first, why are they more deserving, why aren't I as needy? Setting aside consequences for a brief, brief second, it is not really more complicated than when I once confronted my three children with two Oreos and a Saltine. All hell breaks loose. The department made the perfectly practical determination that border states and urban and densely populated areas would have priority over all others. Perfectly practical did not sit well with the kids left with Saltines.

The second challenge facing everyone responding to the H1N1 pandemic was much more difficult. After the vaccines were distributed to each state, decisions then had to be made about how to get them into the arms of citizens. In emergency management, we often call this dilemma "the last mile." We can get things moving in bulk fast, but it is always that last distribution phase where the backup occurs. We knew that decisions made during the last mile had to be made by state and local officials, because they understand their communities. They know how to educate people about where and when to stand in line.

After all, that was the only solution: Everyone would just have to stand in line. And that is where I found myself in the late fall of 2009, at the DC public middle school that had been designated as a flu-shot site. We had received by mail a notification of the day and time—a Saturday morning—and took books and Game Boys to wait it out. Like everyone else, I was just a parent that morning, doing what the plan required: getting my kids a simple shot of a new vaccine that had been created, validated, screened, produced, and distributed as quickly as imaginable, but certainly not as fast as anyone desired.

I knew, as everyone else in that line surely did, that our responsibilities as parents required standing in a line that stretched well outside the school. As every mother certainly knows, we would do anything to keep dangers from entering our home.

But that day was as much about civic duty as it was about my children's health, a gesture to protect all of us. As a mother and an expert, I understood that our children are much more likely to live free from the diseases that have plagued most of mankind because we all get vaccines. One of the attributes of a resilient society is that its citizens accept a certain amount of responsibility for the benefit of, well, living in society. There's a catch: It only works if everyone comes along for the ride.

I simply have little tolerance for the vaccination debate that fills way too much time in parenting discussions. Many activists and parents feel that vaccines are responsible for disorders that befall young babies, including autism. I'm not even sheepish about this issue; there is right and there is wrong here. There should be no debate. I know I'm supposed to be sympathetic, as a mother, about concerns over the side effects of vaccines for our children. I'm not.

I love my children no less than those parents who balk at vaccines love theirs. But I am also equally sure that I love their children just a bit more than they love mine. This assertion can be proven through indisputable statistics. There is negligible evidence that one child might face a permanent and harmful consequence from her exposure to a shot. Anti-vaccination advocates argue that even this (hypothetical) slight risk to a single child outweighs the undeniable benefits to a society that has essentially eradicated viruses that have killed millions. In homeland security terms, they are so focused on the black swan that they are forgetting the greater good.

Based on my professional background and, with three kids, my personal skin in the game, I'm as sanctimonious about this issue as the most zealous critic of vaccination programs. Travel the world—see the consequences when nations do not take public health as seriously as we do—and you will learn that America is resilient against the plagues of the past because we have made much behavior in our society subject to vaccination requirements. It is no wonder that most public health experts were aghast at disclosures that, during the pursuit of Osama bin Laden, the CIA had utilized a Pakistani doctor and a faux vaccination campaign to get access to his compound. After that, Pakistanis began to distrust the vaccination efforts, public health volunteers (and, even more grotesquely, the recently vaccinated) were murdered, and smallpox reemerged as a killer.

We are a strong nation because we take risks that make us collectively stronger. Anyone who doesn't is a free rider. The way I look at it, even assuming a minimal risk of long-term side effects from vaccinations, the only reason why parents can contemplate not vaccinating their child is because they know that the vast majority of citizens will, like me, shoulder that slight risk and put their own children through the recommended course of treatment. But if everyone followed their path, the result would be utterly predictable—our children would be less safe. Period.

Here is the real definition of a security mom: my love for my children doesn't stop at my front door. My children, and my neighbors' children, will prosper in a society where disease has essentially been eradicated. Embracing resiliency is nothing more than taking that leap: get the shot and improve your world—hell, *the* world.

It took two hours, at most, to get the kids vaccinated. When we left, people were still waiting patiently with their children. Even if everyone there was animated by the perfectly selfish decision to make sure his own child was not infected, the fact remained that each vaccinated kid increased the likelihood that we would stop the spread of the virus. The best way to be resilient was to simply and faithfully stand in line. And that is what I did. That is what *we* did.

In the end, H1N1 did not become a public health catastrophe. Some speculated that we had overreacted. Or maybe, just maybe, the response and vaccination program stopped the spread of the virus cold. Sometimes in my field, when the worst doesn't happen, it's about as close to a victory lap as we are ever going to get.

We have a tendency to believe that success and failure are binary options—something either works or it doesn't. A combination of efforts, from vaccines to social distancing to travel restrictions, and maybe even good luck, were factors in our outcome. We can never know what might have happened absent one of them. Success is not always that a good thing happened, but that a bad thing didn't happen quite so badly. So maybe we overreacted. Or maybe we should define success by how well we avoid failure.

SINGLE POINT
OF FAILURE

LIFE AT DHS WASN'T ONE CRISIS AFTER ANOTHER, THOUGH IT COULD FEEL THAT way. In between, there were policy issues related to immigration, funding, and security policies that often slogged along at the normal pace of bureaucratic shifts. Meetings, more meetings, endless meetings, and then more.

With no history, primary issues that were less than inspiring, and a legacy of doubt about our very existence, we at DHS didn't easily fit in with the more established crowds at State or Defense. Even our décor was abysmal; the buildings felt like school trailers. The secretary's personal office—no dramatic murals, no long corridors— paled in comparison to her counterparts'. I sometimes joked that the next secretary of DHS should be Martha Stewart, just so that she could redecorate.

Though we didn't do much with the décor, we managed to alter some of the more egregious policies we inherited. In particular, we rescinded a small but highly controversial program that targeted Arab men entering the country—known as NSEERS, the National Security Entry-Exit Registration System—that caused considerable anger in Arab communities here and abroad. We made less of a dent on broader issues. Comprehensive immigration reform never came during my tenure, despite hopes that it would. And the possibility that Guantánamo Bay detainees might be placed in maximum-security facilities in the United States was thwarted by Congress, responding to legislators' more parochial concerns that an alternative facility might end up in their state.

Work was stressful. I wouldn't say it was fun. Sometimes it was exciting; at other times it was devastating. Progress was difficult to measure, as it always is in disaster management. And the failures were pretty obvious.

In December 2009, I received a phone call from Mark Sullivan, the longtime director of the Secret Service. Sullivan rarely called me. In fact, he never called me. There was never any reason to. So I was filled with some anxiety upon hearing his voice. My assistant even came running into the office, almost gasping. We were both convinced that I had done something wrong. Sullivan has that effect on people.

But he simply needed a favor. There had been a single point of failure, one breach of the security system that brought the whole thing down. And I was his backup plan.

It started with a White House state dinner just a few weeks earlier. Just as the flu season approached and the vaccine distribution campaign was stabilized, the White House had organized a big state party for the prime minister of India. These are lavish affairs, undertaken for only a select few heads of state, often timed for some political statement about continuing partnership between the two countries. Enter Michaele and Tareq Salahi from Virginia, notorious White House party gate-crashers and aspiring stars of the reality show *The Real Housewives of DC*. Uninvited, they managed to get through security and shake hands with the president.

The public and media were horrified by the Salahis' actions. Publicly, I shared this sentiment. Personally, though, I found the Salahis mesmerizing. I'll admit it: I'm a fan. Nothing makes a JetBlue flight go faster than to land upon a *Real Housewives* marathon. My reality—banal disasters at home, actual disasters at the office—is so utterly unlike their reality, except, of course, when the two worlds collide.

The investigation of the gate-crashers exposed some terribly bad judgment on the part of the Secret Service and resulted in a rare apology by Sullivan. An internal review blamed a rushed security line, the annoyance of rain, and Social Secretary Desirée Rogers's decision to move the adjudication of any discrepancies between the invite list and the attendees past the first security line. That decision resulted in a test of wills between a young Secret Service agent and two people who insisted that they were invited.

The Salahis couldn't have predicted what came next: congressional hearings, the threat of a lawsuit, and the eventual departure of Rogers. The Salahis were, in our post-9/11 security culture, not just a joke. They passed through two security checkpoints, including one that absolutely required photo ID. It may have been that they looked the part; after all, Michaele spent a reported seven hours (I just have to wonder out loud what takes seven hours, exactly) at the Erwin Gomez Salon in Georgetown prepping herself before slinking into a gold-embroidered red sari-esque dress. The result: the Salahis eventually got a picture with the president. That, and the Secret Service and DHS became prime fodder for late-night comedians. Oh, and kudos to the Bravo network.

I thought of the first lady. I do not know how she felt about the events of that night, but they proved that her home—even if it is the White House—was vulnerable. That had to be one of the most discombobulating aspects of raising a family at 1600 Pennsylvania Avenue. What if, she had to be thinking. How could the system be so utterly idiotic? I sympathized, even though I was part of that system. It was a serious breach for which there are no excuses. It was a single point of failure.

The dinner incident was remarkable not simply because it happened, but because of how it happened. Systems of security are supposed to have layers and layers of redundancies, backups, and overlaps so that they can withstand or overcome the breakdown of one part and minimize the impact of any deficiencies in planning. In other words, there should never be a single point of failure. One moment—one Secret Service agent who felt pressured not to check the Salahis' identification—simply opened the door to the Obama home. There was no protective net. It was likely an early hint at the systemic deficiencies that would be exposed after it was discovered that Secret Service members were involved in prostitution rings, and later, in separate incidents, failed multiple times to protect the first family from intruders jumping gates to the White House.

The problem for Sullivan was that he had to fix something fast. And that was why he called me. The fifty state governors were coming to the White House as part of the National Governors Association (NGA) meeting the next day. As part of the festivities, there is always a meeting and dinner at the White House with the first couple.

The governors were all staying at the same hotel. Security identification, Sullivan explained, would occur there, at a side door where each governor would be processed and loaded onto a bus, and then the bus would drive straight through the East Wing gates to the White House event. There would be no secondary screening so long as everything went smoothly at the hotel. The event was small enough and the crowd sufficiently elite that the Secret Service had confidence they could protect the president. So long, that is, as there was an exact match between each governor and his or her identification. The governors had been alerted that they needed to withstand additional scrutiny at the hotel. State police or political hacks accompanying a governor could not be used as a form of identification. Everyone knew what had happened at the state dinner and understood.

The problem was that governors tend to be very, very certain that people know who they are. They are not shy about asserting the fact they are the governor, master of their state, a duly elected politician, and, in some instances, the bomb. They may not have the Salahis' sense of entitlement, but they are not used to showing identification.

Because of my role at DHS, I knew most of the governors personally, and those I didn't I could certainly recognize by sight. Sullivan, no fool, understood that if he could convince me to join him at the hotel, I could provide some visual backup. I would probably not be needed, but god help him if this did not go smoothly. And by having a political appointee there with him, he could throw me under the bus should anything go wrong. Like I said, no fool.

Sullivan knew this last part to be true when I called him on it. He laughed and promised me a coffee. I demanded a venti and agreed to meet his team the next morning.

We sipped our coffee and scanned though photos of all the governors. Their official pictures were much better than what I saw in the lobby that day. Sullivan watched as I squinted at a man in cowboy boots. "Perry," I said, "Texas." Schwarzenegger needed no introduction. That guy with the cowboy hat: Schweitzer, from Montana. And so we went through the list as they passed through the real security, a sweep for firearms and a more rigorous identification check. All the governors behaved, as we expected. Sullivan and his agency had learned—no more single points of failure.

I'm invested in this *Real Housewives* saga because it had an unknown second act, one that began with Sullivan and me sipping coffee. This was what we experts call the "feedback loop," the capacity to learn and adapt based on the lessons of past mistakes. Such changes do not need to be dramatic or life-altering: locks on cockpit doors after 9/11, for example. Visual and positive identification was how the Secret Service adapted.

I know blame is appropriate; mistakes are sometimes unforgivable. But to view a security breach solely as the fault of some agent who didn't sufficiently challenge the Salahis—as much as to put the blame for the government's inadequate response to Hurricane Katrina solely at the feet of then FEMA director Michael Brown—is dangerous. It inhibits our capacity to learn from our mistakes and to refocus our efforts so that, next time, we can avoid repeating them. Crises come, do not doubt it, but we don't need to be hobbled by past errors. We must embrace the "feedback loop," learn from our mistakes, and improve. This is an aspect of a resilient society.

As a parent, this concept is easier to grasp. And I am not talking about when our children do something wrong. I am talking about when *parents* do something wrong. Parenting is a constant feedback loop of learning from mistakes, revising our approach, and ultimately getting to some fictitious finish line, which may be no more than reaching the hour at night when the kids are all finally asleep. David and I have long viewed any overarching philosophy of parenting as a luxury. In the words of that National Guard mother—we deal.

As a parent, I have done some stupid things, and I confess this knowing I keep a great deal of company in this regard. Some of these moves have even put my children at risk, starting with the decision I made in 2001 to walk back home after I received that suspicious envelope at the Kennedy School. I once unknowingly locked a sleeping Leo in our Ford Escape with the keys inside and prayed that he didn't wake up before the fire trucks arrived.

But worst of all, through no fault of her own, my nanny, following the routine I had outlined, once dropped Jeremiah off outside the building in which his martial arts classes are held. She did not know that there was no one inside; they were late, as were others, and the teacher had left, thinking the entire class had been no-shows. By the time Jeremiah figured out that he was alone, our nanny was gone. He was now abandoned.

It was our single point of failure.

Jeremiah kept his head. And a few minutes later, a man who had approached my distraught son on the street called to tell me what had happened. I was no more than ten minutes away, but it was a long ten minutes. I rushed and honked and turned down a street where I double-parked and ran the rest of the way. The man was kind, a father himself, and he stepped in to help Jeremiah. He'd made the call. He'd stuck around. Thank god, I thought to myself.

But what if?

What if no one had stopped to help?

What if the wrong sort of someone had come along?

What if?

I don't let myself go there for too long.

We have a few sleepless nights, figure out a way to laugh about it with the kids, and mend our ways so that there won't be a next time. We learn the lesson; then we move on. Because the only value of the big "what if" mistake is that we learn it can never, ever happen twice.

The shock of a major mistake, both in the home and in the homeland, can be muted by integrating its lessons for the next crisis. Sometimes those fixes are small—like a visual inspection, or waiting for at least three minutes before driving off from martial-arts class drop-off—and sometimes they are more consequential. Public safety agencies that protect the homeland are consistently revising, testing, and re-testing their systems in light of a world that is too hard to predict and where the capacity to screw up is large.

Yes, we make mistakes, unforgiveable ones, professional and personal. But what are we supposed to do next? Resiliency is a constant learning curve. The changes we make should create a new baseline for future catastrophes. This "new normal" will eventually be replaced by a newer normal after our response to the next failure exposes further deficiencies. In the struggle for resiliency, there is no finish line. There is only a plan, and a whole lot of learning, followed by a new and better plan. We know this from our personal lives—the mistakes we make, the emergencies we barely prevent, the challenges we confront daily. We can be paralyzed by the "what if "—trust me, I know—or continue forward armed with the lessons of the past.

This feedback loop, past to present, is a central part of disaster response. The public has every right to demand that the government do better. All I can offer is that the pursuit of resiliency is often undertaken in the context of bad mistakes, and worse choices, at the most unpredictable times.

For example: apparently, terrorists don't take Christmas off.

THE SYSTEM WORKED

DURING THE TWO YEARS WE LIVED IN DC, DAVID AND I WERE LARGELY ABSENT from family life. The alternative would have been for me to quit, and that wasn't an option just yet. I had willingly taken on the responsibilities of the job; it wasn't like I didn't know what I was getting into.

This isn't to say the kids went unfed or homework wasn't reviewed and submitted (mostly) on time. Clothes were bought, washed, and replaced. Doctor's appointments were made and kept. David worked incessantly, while my job was incredibly unpredictable. It is fair to say our family frayed around more than just the edges. We relied heavily on my gracious in-laws, Myra and Jerry. We had full-time help. We leaned on friends, neighbors, and teachers. We weren't happy all the time or very often all at once, but we rolled with the tumult. Which is why I am very proud to say: the system worked.

Sometimes it takes a village, but during the years we lived in northwestern DC, it also took a neighbor. Marissa, to be precise. A photographer, Marissa lived next door with her daughter, Daniela. We owe much of our stability during our Washington sojourn, and much of Cecilia's, to Marissa's warm generosity. Cecilia and Daniela would walk to school together, hang out afterward, and play soccer, all while Marissa cooked and helped with homework. She kept Cecilia's spirits up. Daniela loved that three kids had moved in next door, and both houses kept an open-door policy. It would have been hard not to, since our properties were just about a foot apart. Marissa was also a well-known hostess, and never shied from inviting David and me to her parties, where she cooked plate after plate of the most delicious Italian food.

The arrangement wasn't perfect, and the burdens weren't close to fairly distributed. Viewed from one vantage point, I was an overworked mom whose daughter spent a lot of time next door and who took far more than she gave. Marissa never once suggested she got the lesser part of the deal.

Which brings us to Christmas Day 2009. Marissa had invited us (again) to her home. My parents were in town, and the plan was to open gifts at our house and then, after lunch, head next door for more festivities. My work had, surprisingly, eased a little in December. Secretary Napolitano was in California, and I was enjoying the pause in intensity, a momentary calm. As I closed up my DHS office on Christmas Eve, I grabbed a few reports I intended to read, printed out some e-mails that were too difficult to process online, and scoured my office for anything else I might need.

I distinctly remember looking at my classified phone, a device given to senior members in national or homeland security so that they can converse about intelligence when away from secure buildings. Given its purpose, I always thought it should have been encased in fire-truck-red plastic. Of course, it had a dull, ordinary black shell, which belied the fact that it was a highly technical piece of equipment.

A complex sequence of numbers and keystrokes was required to unlock the device, and, with too much negligence, the entire process was easily forgotten. I traveled a lot for the department and never flew without it, but I could count on one hand the times I had heard it ring.

This is Christmas, I thought. The irrational part of my brain argued that during this time of joy and family, even terrorists would surely take a few days off. The rational part of my brain argued that my office was a mere ten minutes away from my home. I could also be inside an ultra-secure SCIF within thirty minutes if need be. Everyone important knew how to get ahold of me via unsecured phone lines, and I could hop into a car at a moment's notice. Anyway, I told myself, no one would ever attack on Christmas. So I left the phone behind.

We are raising our children Jewish, and I have learned, as David explained, that "every Jewish kid complains about Hebrew school. It is guaranteed in the Torah." Still, I negotiated the retention of Christmas. For any interfaith family like ours, we make our traditions as we go along, and they seem to work simply because the kids don't know any different. But the simple fact of the matter is that I'm addicted to Christmas.

I make up for a year of Hebrew school and the kids' impending bat and bar mitzvahs by laying it on thick during the holidays. It is slightly obscene. The kickoff includes an annual run to Target to pick up decorative crap; our house can barely hold the knickknacks that I place on every bookshelf, tabletop, and doorway. David finally drew the line at a Santa Claus toilet seat cover, but that gives you a sense of how bad my addiction is.

And then there is the tree, which, after many years of negotiation, is allowed to exceed seven feet but never pass eight. Somehow seven feet, to David, feels less overwhelming. David grew up eating Chinese food and watching movies on December 25. And so I am grateful that over the years he has let the holiday spirit seep in, finally giving up at seven feet and not much more.

That Christmas morning we followed our usual routine. David and I pretend to sleep in while the kids abide by the "no going downstairs" rule. I make my coffee, David takes a leisurely shower, and we let them simmer in anticipation. Then, at the moment they are about to break, I holler from downstairs that they can join us.

Our kids congregated by the tree, dying to find out who got the best haul. I tend to shop throughout the year and allow them to choose one big gift. On the 23rd of each December, I use the tremendous logistical skills I have honed at work to divvy up the gifts by child, size, and value to ensure that, well, I love all my children equally. One Christmas, when I somehow got the calculation wrong, I was torn between chiding Jeremiah for not being grateful and wondering, deep down, how I could have been so negligent. In 2009, though, I had gotten it just right. The gifts were opened in no time flat, and we bagged the trash and waited for Marissa's party to begin.

It would have been about this time that Umar Farouk Abdulmutallab, a twenty-three-year-old Nigerian man, entered US airspace on Northwest Airlines Flight 253 from Amsterdam Airport Schiphol with 290 passengers on board. Abdulmutallab had managed to embark with plastic explosive devices sewn into his underwear, a fact that would later result in giggles: The kids thought it was so funny that someone put explosives in his underwear. That was much later, though, as was the knowledge that, according to DHS's report, the device was "more incendiary than explosive" and designed to set the plane on fire rather than blow it up.

On December 25, at around 11:25 a.m., a Dutch passenger named Jasper Schuringa heard a pop from the other side of the airplane and essentially flung himself over the aisle to tackle and restrain Abdulmutallab, who had suffered severe burns. The plane landed at 11:53 a.m. in Detroit, where it was immediately guided to a side runway, surrounded by police cars and emergency vehicles, and searched by bomb-disabling robots.

Marissa's party began at noon.

I didn't notice the first few attempts to reach me on my regular cell phone. When I did, the number appeared as the NOC, the National Operations Center. Always on call, it is the office that coordinates the flow of information in a crisis. It holds the name and phone number of anyone who might be needed at a moment's notice; it also knows my home address, David's name and phone numbers, and whether I am in the Washington area or traveling. They knew how to find me, but that Christmas, I didn't know I had to be found.

I called back, but since I hadn't checked my e-mails that day, I hadn't a clue as to what was happening. Had I checked, I would have known that the FAA was assessing the status of every single plane up in the air based on protocols established after 9/11. All were accounted for. I would also have learned that TSA had immediately tightened security on what was normally a low-volume travel day— vacations, and the onslaught of travelers, typically start on the 26th.

Abdulmutallab's was a criminal attack in the homeland; the FBI was the lead agency. Because the attack was unsuccessful, DHS's operational role was pretty minimal. There just wasn't that much to do. We would essentially provide to the bureau's investigators information that would be in our possession, such as travel and airport records. We were also responsible for communicating what our response would be to Detroit, Michigan, and essentially every other nervous governor, mayor, police chief, emergency manager, airport administrator, airline union official, and citizen who might be traveling or about to travel in the next week. But there was, fortunately, no mess to clean up.

I knew none of this at the time I returned the NOC's call. Marissa's home was full of friends and her family, the house rich with the smells of fresh Italian food: baked ham and meatballs covered in sauce. Bowls of licorice and chocolates were plentiful, and I noted, more than once, Leo's hand shoving M&Ms into his pocket. Daniela and the kids spent a lot of time upstairs playing Wii. No one had seen the television all day.

When the NOC operator answered, I told him my name and was patched through to one of the senior lead briefers. Without any fanfare, he simply told me the news: what had happened, what we knew so far, and that a further call was scheduled with the secretary's senior management team to review protocols, statements to the press, and what the department would be allowed to do next.

I say "allowed" because the same procedural dance—ever-escalating conversations about seniority and planning—was being performed all around DC: by the Justice Department, the National Counterterrorism Threat Center, the CIA, the Pentagon and the Defense Intelligence Agency, the Transportation Department and the FAA, and most certainly the White House. Each would be gathering the troops and determining next steps, and then the White House would convene its own secure videoconference to align all the different pieces for one coherent—if we were lucky—response.

The request for the second call came just a few minutes later. It was not classified, but might entail the disclosure of classified information should the need arise. I was without my secure phone and admitted sheepishly that that was the case. A pause. "Get on this call, and then we will see," said the generic NOC administrator.

The secretary was on the phone.

"Merry Christmas, everyone," she bellowed, and the dozen or so people on the phone laughed simultaneously. She was good at finding the dark humor in days that had little of it. "So enough with the whole family-togetherness thing. What have we got?"

The NOC lead read what information was coming in through various public and governmental sources. I couldn't hear a thing. Even somewhat removed from Marissa's gathering—I had stepped into the kitchen to avoid the crowds circulating around the food in the dining room—it was too noisy. There were too many people around. I could have excused myself and walked next door; I could have even gotten into my car to drive the ten minutes to the office. I didn't do either of those things. I wanted to hold onto Christmas so badly.

I escaped to Marissa's first-floor bathroom and crouched in a corner and tried to mute the line for most of the call. Operationally, my role was less to offer input than to soak up everyone else's so I would be able to convey it per the secretary's instructions. TSA security was increased, disclosures to state and local leaders were organized, a separate outreach call to Muslim leaders was scheduled, various intelligence components at DHS were reviewing their records, and we needed to reassure the public that there was no evidence that this was part of a multi-attack plan. We were not, in short, getting ready to upend millions of holiday vacations. We were appropriately focused on the immediate here and now; we were committed to getting the nation back to normal as quickly as possible.

Abdulmutallab was not an idiot, but he was also no sophisticated terrorist. He left clues, if only we had put them together. President Obama would eventually call the missteps in detection "totally unacceptable" and order an investigation. On January 6, 2010, Abdulmutallab was charged by a federal grand jury for the use of a weapon of mass destruction and attempted murder. Two years later, he was sentenced to life in prison without the possibility of parole.

Yes, this was an intelligence failure. Of course it was. As is so often true in these cases, the clarity of hindsight is blinding. But as the terror threat has shifted to solo actors with little contact with organized terror groups, it has limited our capacity to stop someone like Abdulmutallab. During 2009, he spent time in Yemen, Ethiopia, and later Ghana. This journey of radicalization ended with him buying a ticket on December 16, 2009, for a flight from Ghana through Lagos, Nigeria, to Amsterdam, and from there to Detroit. He paid $2,831 in cash, not an unusual form of payment in that part of the world, and also harder to track. On the 24th, he boarded Virgin Nigeria Flight 804 in Ghana. A short stopover later, he was en route to Amsterdam on KLM Flight 588. On the 25th, he was heading to Detroit with a still-undiscovered eighty grams of pentaerythritol tetranitrate (PETN), a crystalline powder, in a six-inch-long plastic container attached to his underwear.

And that is how I ended up sitting on the bathroom floor at a Christmas party. I had forgotten to lock the door. Cecilia must have come downstairs at some point. She found me crouched underneath the sink next to the toilet, phone pressed to my ear.

"What are you doing?" she said, clearly surprised. She immediately realized that the celebration had ended for me. I sharply pointed my index finger to her, signaling "out." It was harsh, unforgiving, but I was on the call with everyone else who had given up on Christmas. To Cecilia's credit, she closed the door quietly.

The phone call ended. There would be others that day, hundreds perhaps, reflecting a government response that swung quickly into action once the intelligence failure was discovered. I soon left Marissa's, explaining to my hostess that I had to go back home and deal with some work issues. I went online. Out of my Christmas daze, it took me just a few minutes to get totally up to speed, reading through DHS e-mails and scanning public news sources. We worked through the day and into the night as various teams were established to deal with the response and with communications. The president was in

Hawaii, and John Brennan, his homeland security advisor, was the White House lead. Secretary Napolitano became the public face of the cabinet, assuring travelers and the public that this was, as far as we knew, an isolated incident and that while security was going to be more intense, the airports would be open.

I thought Christmas was ruined for sure, though an unsuccessful attack is surely better than the alternative. I spent the rest of the day on the phone explaining to folks in Michigan what we knew. Detroit is home to a large Arab and Muslim community, so civil rights teams from Justice and Homeland Security reached out to community contacts to minimize the likelihood of any retaliatory events. We provided intelligence briefings to senior leadership personnel in every state, all of whom were being hounded by the media about whether citizens should board their flights. By then we knew this was an isolated, though scary, event, and our advice was consistent and measured. We urged political, civic, and religious leaders to help the nation remain calm and even festive during the days ahead. We were taking this seriously, but we also didn't want to derail the holidays or curb the economy during the season. And I planned on adhering to this advice myself. I'd reclaim the holiday, somehow.

The kids had returned from Marissa's house, exhausted from a day that began so early and with so much anticipation—until, that is, incendiary underpants over the Midwest had managed to shove the day off-kilter.

"Are we still leaving town tomorrow?" Cecilia asked, fearing that our first vacation away from DC would be interrupted. She knew it wasn't just a question of whether the airports would be open. It was whether her mother, who willfully had taken this job, might be allowed to travel.

"Yes, of course, honey. There isn't anything more for me to do here. Crisis averted," I explained.

She wasn't mollified. "But then there will be another one, and another one," she said. "There always is."

She was right, in more profound ways than she might have imagined. Even in these pre-ISIS days, the nature of the terrorist threat had changed since 9/11. It was now men who were barely ten years old on September 11, 2001; who did not know or fight with bin Laden; who were radicalized quickly, in a manner inconsistent with the deliberative planning of Al Qaeda; who were just like Abdulmutallab. And while that meant that their attacks were more benign than the carefully orchestrated 9/11 attack, it meant also that they were harder to detect in all the intelligence noise. It was like Whac-A-Mole. Success would be measured by how many attacks were victimless, or simply delayed. Just a few months later, another attack was thwarted by a vendor who noticed smoke coming from a car in New York City's Times Square and notified the police.

By late in the evening on the 25th, it was pretty obvious I could continue on with my life. I was nonessential. This distinct Washington complaint stems from the fact that it is the natural inclination of highly ambitious people to want to be at the center of decision making, and, not infrequently, the center of attention. When you work for the government, you are well aware of the pecking order (assistant secretary is under an undersecretary, despite the name confusion).

By the morning of the 26th, I had directed my staff to cover any additional requests and managed to retrieve my classified phone. My family and I headed out, leaving for the airport extra early because of the increased security. Unlike when traveling for work, I actually prefer to overpack with kids in tow. I learned early as a parent that committing to inefficiency is much less stressful than trying to pack with precision. We checked some luggage. Depending on what we had in our carry-ons, from books to Game Boys, we bowed to varying degrees when making our way to the security checkpoint. Predictably, the line stretched in and around and around again.

As a civilian working in public safety, I had a badge as well. I always thought it was unnecessary, but—like the state trooper car—I understood why. In an emergency, it could make a profound difference. But like the car so many years ago, it might just offer a sort of temptation to make my personal life easier at the worst of moments. The temptation was great when I saw that long line at the airport.

"Is this because of you?" Leo asked as we waited at the back. It was accusatory more than anything else, like *you caused this* (which I didn't), *so get us out of this* (which I couldn't). Lines, for any child, are a form of purgatory, and I have childlike tendencies when I enter any airport.

My children believe—honestly believe—that they have two mothers. The first is me: somewhat fatalistic, always hopeful, and able to balance a lot of chaos. And then there is the scary version of me, otherwise known as, in Cecilia's terms, "Airport Mom." Airport Mom is stressed, cruel, cranky, and short-tempered. Delays are taken personally, lines are a form of torture, and the children are under constant threat of verbal abuse should things go wrong. David sometimes jokes around on the drive to the airport as if Airport Mom were a ghost: "Is she with us yet? Go into the light. Stay away."

Airport Mom was alive and well that December day, tempted by the badge in her purse, so tired from the day before, mentally exhausted by the dramatic shift from gift giving to attempted terrorist attack, and by looking at a line that was the result of a security apparatus on higher alert.

Leo and Jeremiah stayed well away from Airport Mom. I could hear them giggling. "It's because of the underwear guy," Leo told his little brother, as both burst out laughing. So did Cecilia. "Come on, Mom," she said, "it is *kind of* funny." It wasn't, but the kids could make it so. They were fine, we were fine, and the airplanes kept moving. So, too, did the line. The system was adapting.

The following week at the beach was quiet. So it came as a surprise to see Secretary Napolitano on television, from her vacation in California, remarking about the incident that "the system worked." It was clearly a talking point, the same kind of talking point that is demanded often by political communications teams, but is not really thought through for how it will actually sound when it comes out of an administration official's mouth.

Napolitano meant that the system worked if you judge it from the moment that Abdulmutallab tried to light himself on fire. A passenger responded quickly. The pilot notified the control tower. The suspect was isolated and detained until the flight arrived. Law enforcement officials surrounded the plane. Every plane in the air was assessed for any security risk. Relevant parties were notified. The suspect was taken into custody. There was an immediate press conference. The system worked!

But in the public's eyes, Abdulmutallab should never have gotten on that plane. The reaction to Napolitano's comments led some to call for her resignation.

Now that I'm out of government, I can say what I couldn't then. Our world is interconnected and fluid. There are millions of people getting on and off airplanes every moment of every day. The TSA is by no means perfect, but the folks charged with keeping air travel safe are doing everything they can; sometimes the dots aren't connected, or there are too many dots, and we just can't guarantee that some violent extremist, who might have otherwise been an isolated misfit but for a chance meeting with radicals in Yemen, won't try to light his underwear on fire. Our system is porous to the likes of Abdulmutallab because we need it to be.

I can't forgive the intelligence failures that led to the Christmas surprise. Still, the system "worked" because the public was involved, because passengers and airline security and the pilots and the FAA and the FBI and hundreds of others, on their Christmas Day, all reacted when they were needed most. We become so focused on placing blame for the potential catastrophe, we risk failing to nurture all aspects of the response that helped avoid it.

I'd like to believe that, one day, there will be peace on earth for my children, but I know that my wishing can't make it so. The only thing I can do, as an expert and as a mom, is to participate in a society that prevents violence as much as possible and responds quickly when it can't prevent it. The system worked simply because the worst-case scenario was averted.

THE KIDS AREN'T ALRIGHT

FROM THAT CHRISTMAS ON, I ALWAYS KEPT MY CELL PHONE AND MY SATELLITE phone nearby. They replaced the baby monitor on my bedside table. One night in January 2010, a persistent ring woke me up.

"Is this Juliette?" a male voice asked.

"Yes. Who is this?" I said.

"Governor Rendell. It's about Haiti." I knew exactly what he was talking about. A few days before, on January 12, an earthquake that reached 7.8 on the Richter scale had devastated that nation, killing over two hundred thousand people.

"Can you hold on a second, Governor?" I whispered as I looked over at David. He was up now, and gestured as to whether he should leave the room. "It's Rendell," I whispered to him. He nodded and gave me a smile. I scrambled for sweatpants and a sweater. Another night lost for us, but David needed his sleep. Another night lost, but we were used to it.

Government work had not been easy on us, despite the fact that we had braced ourselves for the demands of our jobs. We were always a team. I do not know of a time in my adult life when David was not part of it. We met in college, dated for a brief while, broke up and dated other people, and then reintroduced ourselves in law school. I have been with him longer than I have been without him. He defines my adult life. David is now a federal circuit court judge and disfavors public attention. He appears in this book more than he would like and less than he should. If he seems to play only a supporting role, it is only because that is what I owe him for being my primary support.

We are very different. He is calm and cerebral, while I am more outgoing and social. That combination makes a lot of sense; it always made a lot of sense even when we weren't together. When I returned from a year in South Africa after college to attend law school in 1992, I hadn't spoken to David since 1990, after our college breakup. Nevertheless, one of the first phone calls I made was to his sister to find out where he was. I don't remember why I did this, only that I knew he, too, was at Harvard Law School and that I thought I'd better let him know I would be arriving there, a graduation year behind him.

He jokes that my decision to call him showed that I always regretted our breakup. In the scheme of such a long marriage, our few years apart don't mean much. During that respite, I dated a business school guy who would later become a multimillionaire; whenever I complain about our 2003 Ford Escape, David always says, "You could have married James." There was, later, a white South African doctor who seemed, when I was twenty-two, charming and complicated but who, upon further reflection, was clearly just screwed up. Meanwhile, David was with a woman who was only *half* Lebanese, which I took to mean if he couldn't have the real deal, he'd settle.

So when I returned to Cambridge for law school, David and I planned to meet for lunch. A truce, I guess. I opened the door to my new apartment and there he stood, as handsome as I remembered. We hugged, awkwardly. He didn't say much. I excused myself to finish getting ready, claiming my hair was still wet when he could easily tell that it wasn't. Alone in the bathroom, I started hyperventilating and tried to brace myself. This wasn't over. I knew exactly why I had called him. There were a few short weeks of pretending that we were not going to be together again, and then, seemingly in a flash, we were engaged, married, pregnant, pregnant again, pregnant once more, and it was 2010.

Our years in Washington weren't ideal, the stresses of work life and home life making each other easy targets. Our rented house was too small, our bedroom had too few closets, our time together was too neglected—we rarely had time for dinner together, let alone a movie. David's job was so different from mine: more consistently intense and with more homework, a constant stream of opinions to research and write. David was more often than not arriving home way past the kids' bedtimes. I resented him at times, feeling that the burdens of the stress in the family fell disproportionately on me. Of course, those burdens—it is very fair to say—equal out over the years of a marriage, each person picking up the slack when need be. This fact is easily forgotten by the burdened parent in the midst of combat duty.

So it wasn't easy. Period. We avoided the conversation about what all this was doing to our family and our marriage. There was no room for sentimentality. We knew these jobs were time-limited. Our marriage shouldn't be. We would survive interrupted nights of sleep.

That night was one such night, though the Haiti earthquake was like no other. Every major television station beamed images of a major city flattened by force. They broadcast the sounds of desperate pleas for help from those still buried. The earthquake devastated a nation that has had more than its fair share of horror and tragedy. Over the previous few days in January, I had watched the images broadcast out of Haiti as I joined the department's hastily convened Haiti response team. I focused on the earthquake's potential impact on the homeland, if there should be one. Initially, that meant working with the Defense Department should Haitian patients have to come to the United States. We needed to organize a fair distribution of the burden throughout public hospitals in each of the states.

The earthquake had destroyed the Haitian government's infrastructure, and in all practicality there was no functioning government there. But it still was a sovereign nation. We would have to balance our desire to help with the recognition that Haiti was not—despite all of our previous forays into the country during the twentieth century—our nation to run.

The United States' help was sorely needed. Setting aside relative proximity, no one could come close to providing the array of assets that America could. FEMA has the most sophisticated federal search-and-rescue capacity in the world, the military (most important, the navy) can transport resources and personnel to stabilize and assist with medical needs, and the Coast Guard can help protect the waters and guide boats delivering food and water. We have doctors, and nurses, and medical facilities, and all sorts of gear and goods and technology to help those in need.

America may be guilty of initiating wars with no justification, but we are also a tremendously generous nation. As the world's greatest power, it is our responsibility to help others; I now believe it is also our inclination. In the days after the earthquake, a massive humanitarian effort was set in place. It would include various agencies at DHS, FEMA and the Coast Guard in particular, who worked with the State Department's USAID (United States Agency for International Development), which serves as the lead agency for foreign disasters. There were also a lot of American citizens interested in what was going on in Haiti, including a Pennsylvania governor known as much for his impatience as for his unquestioning compassion.

"What the hell is going on with the orphans?" he asked over the phone, and I knew exactly what he was talking about. Those children. My heart ached when I saw the pictures and videos of so many abandoned kids during those days. There were just too many of them, too many left alone.

Many of those children were in orphanages well before the earthquake and were supposed to be en route to new, caring homes outside of Haiti, including in the United States. In some instances, they were as close as getting on a plane, with all the appropriate papers completed, to their new families in America. In other instances, they were midway through the process, a few papers left undone. Those children, still in Haiti, were now joined by god knows how many new orphans created by the earthquake.

We faced a dilemma. Disaster management, at home or overseas, is always about logistics. An effective plan requires a clear sense of how to move goods, supplies, and people to save lives and protect property. We have to choose. It is a form of triage that takes place every day in hospital trauma wards: How do we save as many lives as possible, how do we decide who goes first into the operating room, how do we set priorities?

In the case of these orphans, the United States couldn't just take them, regardless of what our hearts told us to do. Nations are very clear that rules and procedures need to be followed. No matter what the reason or how bad things look, foreign governments cannot just go in and rescue orphaned kids.

Rendell knew this, clearly. Several American missionaries had just been arrested in Haiti for trying to take children—children they claimed were orphans, but Haiti claimed were not—to the Dominican Republic, where it was safer. Rendell's concern was different: several Pennsylvania families were so close to finalizing adoptions in Haiti that it seemed a strange form of cruelty to keep the children there, tied up on a technicality that would not be easily resolved, given that all the paperwork was probably lost.

"We've got to speed up this process. Make it right. We've got the families here already," he implored, minutes past midnight. The problem was more fundamental than just speed. Haiti was still a sovereign nation. They were still in charge. We could not just take babies, claiming they would be better off elsewhere, despite the fact that it might look that way.

That is not a message that is easy to deliver. Rendell was not happy on that call, nor should he have been. I told him what I knew at the time: Efforts were already under way to provide some flexibility in the adoption process for children with families anticipating their arrival. I explained that the White House had already deployed top staff to Haiti solely to facilitate this process. "It's really complicated," I told him.

I remember him ending the call with the simplest of replies: "It's really not that complicated."

But it was. Cold as this sounds, cold as I sound, the kids would have to wait. The media, disappointed would-be parents, and health and social service agencies would all focus on the government's slow response delivering adopted kids out of Haiti. This is one of the incongruities between what is required of disaster management and how it is perceived: The priorities regarding what needs to get done first can often look misaligned. Governor Rendell's focus on getting the children out, and addressing the needs of his citizens, was just one of several priorities. Sometimes decisions don't always cater to the heartstrings: bluntly, it isn't always about the children. In Haiti, our goal was to save the nation first. There was no room for sentimentality.

The challenge in Haiti had nothing to do with motivation or desire, or even competency. It had to do with a runway; it's as simple as that. What people didn't understand as they clamored for more doctors or child-care specialists or relief workers was that the real dilemma was about getting stuff—basic stuff—to an island that was isolated. People, goods, food, water, shelter must move quickly and reliably. These logistics are always the foundational priority. Without them, no effort can last for long. Alexander the Great famously remarked that "My logisticians are a humorless lot . . . they know if my campaign fails, they are the first ones I will slay." He wasn't joking.

In Haiti, Mother Earth's cruelty came by land and by sea, killing people, destroying property, and devastating the ports. But she did not arrive by plane; the airport runway near Port-au-Prince was spared. If there was any mercy in Haiti in January 2010, it was that a single transportation lane was somehow left alone. One sole landing strip unscathed at the Toussaint Louverture International Airport provided Haiti's lifeline to the outside world. But only one.

That first night after the earthquake, Haiti's only seaport was damaged, and no ships could approach the nation to deliver goods. A single dangerous lane of road could be driven from the Dominican Republic, but that trip was over ten hours long. The airport—the only feasible point of entry—stayed quiet. There was no air traffic control, no tower communications, no navigational or landing aides.

When morning came, the US Air Force did a fly-by and determined that the airport could handle the rush of aid. Secretary of State Hillary Clinton convinced then Haitian president René Préval to cede operations to the US military. Given the history of American military involvement in Haiti, including the entry of US forces in 1994 to reinstate President Jean-Bertrand Aristide—during Bill Clinton's presidency, no less—Secretary Clinton's request was not received warmly. But Préval was well aware of his country's isolation and its pressing needs. He had no other choice.

A plastic folding table and some chairs were set up in the grass next to the runway. There was no electricity, no computers, not even telephones. There was also no space for long goodbyes; the airport could park only twelve planes. Regimented time slots were provided to incoming flights. Unloading happened quickly. The first priority was getting substantial amounts of goods safely in, offloaded, and catalogued.

The airport normally received twenty-five flights a day. During the twelve days after the earthquake, it would manage 2,222 airplanes and an additional 800 helicopters with only handheld radios to guide them in. Relief was coming, managed by a system less sophisticated than a fourth grader's playroom.

There was one airfield, one single runway. So the order of supplies and personnel arriving at the airport needed to be prioritized. Haiti's government had singled out food and water as its top needs. Water and food: that is what saves lives. This also led to what seemed like a cruel act—initially favoring the twenty thousand US troops who could set up a food and water supply system—that led the France-based NGO Doctors Without Borders to publicly complain that it couldn't get enough of its medical professionals into the country.

There was also a second and much more self-interested aspect to our focus on food and water. We were invested in restoring order in Haiti because if Haitians did not have access to these basic necessities, they might take to the oceans and try to save themselves. It had happened before, in 1991, when hundreds of thousands took to boats to flee political unrest.

Homeland security is as much about offense as it is about defense. A primary part of my responsibility in the Haitian response revolved around the concern that the United States might face a mass migration. As I had learned when we first discussed that fateful snow day in Massachusetts, and again when we orchestrated the campaign to develop, produce, and distribute a vaccine in response to the H1N1 virus, we must always prepare for the worst-case scenario. The purpose of our foreign assistance to a place like Haiti has strong moral backing. But we delude ourselves if we think that ensuring the safety and security of our neighbors is purely altruistic. If Haitians in their thousands got into boats and started heading to the United States, more lives would be at risk in the tumultuous waters. It would also create a different political crisis on the home front.

The scenarios for a mass migration are never good, especially for Haitians. Because of laws that favor Cuban refugees, those who flee Havana and can get even a single foot on US soil are given lawful status; this is known as the "wet foot/dry foot" rule. It is a reflection of our sympathies for those who live under Castro and a rule that seems increasingly antiquated in this post–Cold War era, a fact later recognized by President Obama when he opened diplomatic relations with Cuba in 2015. Regardless, for Haitians captured in our waters or who actually reached the coast, the options were pretty horrible: either a detention facility in Florida or one on Guantánamo Bay. Yes, *that* Guantánamo.

Guantánamo is a United States military prison, which holds detainees—all foreign—captured in the war on terror. It possesses a foul, horrific legacy; Obama's promises to close it have been stymied by other nations' unwillingness to take back their citizens and domestic laws that make closing it impossible. It is a shameful blight on our nation.

JULIETTE KAYYEM

But Guantánamo is also, on the other side of the naval base, a holding facility for refugees from the Caribbean. Still, the idea that we would take Haitians fleeing a tragedy to the same place where we hold terror suspects was not going to be politically acceptable. We knew that. Nor, in the context of domestic politics, would be assigning them to detention centers in Florida. The best we could do at the time was to invoke temporary protected status (TPS) for any Haitian immigrants in the United States who had to return to Haiti because their visas expired or they were under court order. We suspended any obligation that they return, knowing that during those early months after the earthquake we could not force people back to a nation in crisis. The administration made that announcement when I accompanied Napolitano and Vice President Joe Biden to Miami to meet with members of the Haitian community, who were very worried about their families back home. I had never traveled with the vice president; I remember driving with him into the city from the airport and thinking how light the traffic was, until I realized the freeway had been closed for his entourage.

The Haiti response had so many inherent stresses, based on so many capacity limitations, that the administration began to resemble a family with all its tensions. Each agency and department has its own strong and essential priorities and equities; we are rarely one big happy family. At one stage during the response, I convened a meeting for the State Department at which we discussed the Coast Guard's plans in the event of a potential mass migration. I explained how the Coast Guard was monitoring from the sky, looking for any evidence of downed trees or movement near water that would suggest a mass exodus. Five Coast Guard cutters were circling the island. Every day, an air force cargo plane flew over the nation, conveying this sad audio message from Haiti's ambassador to Washington, Raymond Joseph: "Listen, don't rush onto boats to leave the country. If you do that, we'll all have even worse problems. Because I'll be honest with you: If you think you will reach the US and all the doors will be wide open to you, that's not at all the case." The message was brutal, I know. It warned every mother and father that whatever their parental inclination to get their child to a safer place, that effort would not work.

At the meeting, Hillary Clinton's top staff and lawyers cringed when we introduced the backup plan: that Guantánamo's holding facility was ready should the need arise. There were moments when my job could be hateful. This was one of them.

"The president just won't accept Guantánamo as an option," one of Clinton's lawyers said to the Coast Guard captain in charge, invoking the commander in chief as if he had spoken to him directly on this issue.

I had to interject. "Do you have better options? A refugee crisis in Florida doesn't seem so ideal from the president's perspective, either." There were no good options except one: Haiti had to be stabilized, even if choosing that priority meant that the orphaned children would not get out immediately.

Sometimes, the least terrible outcome is the only target to shoot for. When a disaster strikes, the primary goal of the response is to stabilize the situation so that recovery—including reestablishing the adoption process—can begin sooner. Triage can look heartless, and it is. It is the language of priorities: first this, then that. But given one runway, it isn't clear that efforts putting adoptive parents first would have been best for the nation—Haiti or America.

Explaining these decisions sounded so technical. There was no room for tears, no time to say that yes, we wanted to help the kids first, too. And so, as I was too often forced to do, I put my feelings aside. I presented our limited options in the objective language of disaster management. I tried not to think too much about it.

Just don't think about it too much. It was easy, or at least familiar. I was doing the same at home: Just get through the day. With our own family under stress, albeit voluntary, I found practical, unemotive ways to master our family's priorities. Maybe it is why I, like so many other mothers I know, find such pleasure in the yellow sticky note. Sometime during my adult life, these helpful little devices became a favorite way to organize a daily rundown, communicate with family, and make lists and more lists (revised on new sticky notes if need be). When the kids are asleep but I've forgotten to ask them something and remembered it only late at night, I'll leave a note on their backpack that says, "Remind me to remind you of something." I learned to approach my own family as a logistical challenge.

I know there is no sentimentality in any of this. There are times when all we can do is hold on and manage, like a nation with one runway or a marriage with too little downtime. Sometimes a good day is simply when each tired sticky note has finally been crumpled into the wastebasket, a legacy of the day past, and at least we've managed to buy ourselves enough wiggle room to surmount the current crisis or heartache and move on to the next day.

THANK YOU FOR YOUR SERVICE

"WE'VE GOT A GAME CHANGER," COAST GUARD REAR ADMIRAL MARY LANDRY remarked to those of us in the administration beckoned to an early-Saturday-morning phone call in late April 2010. Calling from Louisiana, she had mastered the art of delivering bad news in a calm voice, so the gravity of what she was telling us took a moment to seep in. "We believe the blowout preventer did not function. There is oil spilling into the ocean."

Eleven men were dead following an April 20 explosion on British Petroleum's offshore rig in the Gulf of Mexico. That was bad enough, but when the rig ultimately sank and an allegedly fail-safe blowout preventer had, actually, failed, it looked like a whole ocean might be lost.

The mechanics of the spill were pretty simple: A vacuumlike

device was drawing up oil from the ground, and no one had any means of turning it off. The device's tubing was ripped and shredded. Day after day after day, oil gushed into the ocean. We could address the consequences of this crisis by trying to capture the oil, dispersing it with chemicals, burning it on the ocean's surface, or collecting it onshore, but the only way to end it was clear: We had to plug the well.

Landry explained how the Coast Guard, who led DHS's response in this crisis, would deploy resources, or "surge assets." We were going to move a whole lot of people, gear, dispersants, and boats—also known as a whole lot of stuff—to stop the oil and pick up the mess. BP—now a public enemy—was an integral part of the response, since it alone had the technological know-how to fix the well and, pursuant to federal law, would have to pay for all response resources. Landry had already established a command center in Robert, Louisiana, and BP was there. So were local responders from the state.

My involvement with the spill was not preordained, nor even, if you want to get technical, part of my docket. I can never say I was grateful for the crisis, but I can say that, without question, my proximity to managing the chaos in the field profoundly shaped my understanding of homeland security.

Former House speaker Tip O'Neill once said that all politics are local. It is true, and it also applies to oil spills. All disasters are local: really, really local. And that was the least of the lessons learned. By the end of the spill, I would make twenty-five trips to the Gulf, oversee seventy federal agencies, all with some equities in the spill response, serve as the point person for the five impacted statehouses and their governors, attend twice-weekly White House Situation Room meetings, be yelled at, yell in turn, and learn to like scotch.

How did I end up here? I had been told by Secretary Napolitano and then Coast Guard Commandant Thad Allen to leave for Louisiana the day after Landry's phone call. My experience with local and state first responders, as well as with the politics of any disaster, made me uniquely suited for this assignment. I could speak the language of the Coast Guard, the White House, and Louisiana (I was weakest on this last one). I knew Allen, through an ironic twist of fate. Earlier that spring, the Coast Guard had tested their response and recovery protocols in a simulated crisis exercise. This is normal for public safety agencies; they are constantly, and rightfully, testing and retesting their assumptions. Napolitano was busy during the test, so I had attended as the most senior political appointee available to represent the administration. Allen and I spent that afternoon together, him as the command authority, me as the demanding (but never avoidable) political appointee. The exercise was fortuitous: it was based on a fictitious oil spill off the coast of New England.

Allen knew, without having to be told, what was about to unfold. He had managed Hurricane Katrina after FEMA's Michael Brown was fired. There would be blame, and bad press, and a disaster to stop. He also knew from experience that this order was almost impossible to circumvent: first blame, then lots and lots of bad press, and then a resolution. And how we navigated the first two steps had a lot to do with how quickly the underlying cause of the disaster could be addressed.

I arrived in Robert, a small town off the interstate that was only a few miles from the water. An incident command had already been established. All the different pieces of the organized response—logistics, communications, cleanup, finance, shelter, etcetera—shared the same space, a huge, abandoned warehouse. It already had a cafeteria, showers, and a laundry room. Robert was the hub from which orders were directed to various sites throughout the Gulf states where mini–incident commands were stationed. In the end we even outgrew Robert, and the central command moved to New Orleans, directing information and materials to mini-commands in Texas, Louisiana, Mississippi, Alabama, and Florida. And this didn't even include BP headquarters in Houston, where the engineering team focused solely on closing the well. Houston was off-site and out of sight. In Houston, they were already trying everything: domes and wells, filters and robots—just about anything that might work. We had to let them do their job. They were the only ones who could.

In Louisiana, it was eerily calm. Sometimes that can be a helpful attitude in a time of crisis, but here it was also a problem. The public, perhaps rendered familiar with disasters courtesy of film director Michael Bay, wanted to witness a sense of urgency and intensity. They also clamored for a villain. As I had seen throughout the response to Hurricane Katrina, we like to find someone to blame. It was impossible, from our operational standpoint, to throw BP under the bus. Yes, publicly, BP would be the villain, but within the confines of the response, they were our partners in this effort, deploying resources and money to end this abysmal environmental disaster. I don't say this to apologize for BP's actions, only to explain the complexity of our relationship with them. Friend and foe, all wrapped up in one. The ultimate frenemy.

The spill already dominated headlines: neighboring states—aware that water and oil know little of geopolitical boundaries—were demanding we help; Mexico was nervous; England's prime minister (the B is for British, after all) was anxious about the economic viability of a large company whose welfare affected a significant number of public pensions. I was fielding calls from the White House and DHS, a spy of sorts: What were we doing? What was up with BP? Was the Coast Guard ready? Did you hear what Governor Jindal just said? Who the hell put a twentysomething cadet on MSNBC's *Rachel Maddow Show?* I was alone out there among the responders and the oil, reporting back.

On Monday night, after only a day there, I went in search of a space where I could collect my thoughts. I sat outside the command, near midnight, finding solace in the silence. Doug Suttles, BP's chief coordinator for the response, sat down next to me and handed me a beer. He confessed that he came from four generations of oilmen.

"I've never seen anything like this before," I said.

"No one has. This is different. This isn't some ship leaking. This is the ocean. And once the oil hits the shore, well, you haven't seen the South yet."

"You know that none of us is likely to survive this intact," I responded.

"If we go down, you guys go down, too," he laughed. "You'll discover that soon enough. This is oil country. This is your problem as much as ours."

He was right. It was oil country. And it was fish country. The spill devastated the region. Immediately after the BP rig went down, the administration put a moratorium on all offshore drilling because the safety of the other rigs was unknown. So until the moratorium was lifted, no oil was being pumped from the Gulf. At the same time, because the waters were contaminated from the ever-growing oil spill, an entire swath of the Gulf was closed to commercial fishing. The risk that fish turned toxic by oil would enter into the food supply chain was too great. It also meant that every Gulf state was angry— and they weren't just blaming BP. We were the Obama administration, after all.

Later that week, on Thursday, Allen met me at a small airfield with Jindal and his staff, a rough-and-tumble Louisiana crowd— Stetson-wearing, booted men who looked like the kind of folks who hadn't had much use or affection for the federal government for, well, over a century. I was the only woman on the flight, and they eyed me warily for any number of reasons: politics, skin color, last name, gender. But I was more focused on what might seem like a less pressing fact: I had discovered that no amount of product would tame my hair in the Louisiana humidity. It was vanity, but a work-related vanity; I looked like a mess. I twisted and pinned up and rolled my dark and unmanageable mane, but to no avail. In the potential battles ahead with state politicians, I worried that I would not look the part of an intimidating adversary.

At the meeting, we discussed that the oil was appearing in large quantities on the surface of the ocean, five miles from shore. Local politicians wanted to eyeball (and be able to tell their constituents that they had eyeballed) our response efforts at sea. From the airplane's windows, I saw an oil sheen that stretched to the horizon. It was massive. No, it was jaw-dropping. We could see skimmers and other response boats at work, but they seemed insignificant given the amount of oil already spreading out over the waves. Jindal was gracious, but he looked discouraged, as we all did. His entire team stopped joking around and just stared out the window. The magnitude of what we saw hit us all immediately. Oil was spilling into the ocean, at quantities that were unprecedented, and no one knew how to close the well.

Allen and I landed back in Louisiana and then immediately took a Coast Guard flight to meet with Alabama's governor, Bob Riley. Riley was a man with a chip on his shoulder when it came to disasters; his state suffered great damage in Hurricanes Katrina and Rita, but received nothing like the attention given to Louisiana and Mississippi. "I've got six miles of the most gorgeous, uninterrupted beach on this coastline. Summer is coming soon. I already know I need help."

The Alabama governor's message received, we landed at a small airport on the Gulf in his home state. Allen and I then took a short flight together to Mobile, after which I planned to head home. We sat alone at the back of the plane, strategizing.

"This is going to be bad," Allen said matter-of-factly, as he often does. "Really bad. And these guys don't have much love for Obama."

I thought of Jindal and Riley. "It strikes me," I said, unsure of Allen's politics, "that these guys have *no* love for Obama."

All of the Gulf governors were Republicans. Jindal and Mississippi's Haley Barbour would make overtures to run against Obama in 2012; Texas's Rick Perry would eventually enter that crowded race. While it was still two years away, the Republicans had already started to fight for the primary. Allen knew the election calendar. "What," he asked, "are the chances this will have anything to do with an oil spill by the end?"

I said goodbye to Allen and waited for a plane to New Orleans, the first leg of a journey that would take me home after five days away. I had kept up with the kids by phone and e-mail, sending them pictures of the oiled ocean. This was a short trip. The only stress on the family was that I had left in a hurry. They were used to me being gone, but normally they had some notice.

A young Coast Guard cadet approached me on the Alabama tarmac and said, "We need to get you back to Louisiana."

"Under whose orders?" I asked, unsure of what to make of a kid in uniform telling me I couldn't go home.

"Everyone's," he said, with no sense of humor.

After the flyovers, Allen had recommended that the president designate the response a spill of national significance (SONS). This designation, not unlike an emergency declaration, would change the way the response was structured. A SONS had never been declared in US history.

I was utterly unprepared. Unbeknownst to me, I had been tapped to direct both the interagency and intergovernmental efforts for the SONS. Allen had essentially already decided my fate, long before I walked out onto the tarmac.

The job would require me to manage the couple dozen federal agencies that had strong equities in the impact of the spill but that were not necessarily tied directly to the oil spill response itself. A great example is the State Department; it isn't a response agency, but we would need its contacts and trained staff in Mexico should the oil wash up on foreign shores. They were also very concerned about the water current sending oil to Cuba, a nation with whom we then had no ties and no shared protocols. Indeed, multiple agencies and departments would have similar equities—say, the Department of Commerce, given the economic turmoil in the Gulf, or the Food and Drug Administration, which is the only agency that can authorize the reopening of closed contaminated waters after the food supply chain is determined to be clean.

Allen also wanted me to deal with the "GOBIs." It was one of his favorite terms. Technically, it is an acronym for "General Officer Bright Idea," and reflects the military's tendency to do whatever comes out of the mouth of a senior officer. For example, a general officer might say casually, "Those doors would look really good if they were painted yellow." And the next day, they would be yellow. Allen had experienced a variation on that: When any disaster happens, everybody else thinks that you have no idea what you're doing and that only he or she can solve the problem. These GOBIs believe that if only they were in charge, the whole thing would be smooth sailing.

With something like an oil spill, there are a lot of GOBIs. The hairdresser who believes his stylist's spray is a better dispersant than what we are using to clear the oil. The farmer who believes that goat hair can pick up the oil better. The garage-based inventor who believes that if we cut a submarine in half and put it over the blowout preventer, we could collect all the oil better. The list goes on. And all of these people seem to know someone who is the brother-in-law of the dog walker for the daughter of a congressman. And so they all have to be managed. Even the actor Kevin Costner's team from his disastrous film *Waterworld* got an audience with the White House. "Manage the GOBIs," Allen said. And then he laughed, because I had no idea what he was talking about yet.

I reported to Allen, the head of the Coast Guard, who was given the title of national incident commander, a designation he held even after his four-year tenure as Commandant of the Coast Guard expired. I was expected to spend the late spring and summer of 2010 in the Gulf states or in the Situation Room. And not at home.

Armed with a new wardrobe bought from Target, since I hadn't packed much when I first left, I briefly returned to DC eight days later. I somehow managed to sneak in a visit to Jeremiah's "Celebration of Mother Nature" at his school. The preschool's walls were covered with indecipherable crayon etchings of suns and whales and what appeared to be little poodles (sheep?), all symbols of what is good on the Earth. Think rainbows and green trees and majestic (for the four-year-old set) mountain ranges. Here was arrayed tangible evidence of the hopes and pleasures enjoyed by children whose parents have normal jobs. In their midst was Jeremiah's drawing, clearly recognizable as an ocean, with a big black circle spreading out along the bottom of the page. It wasn't clear if his excessive use of grays and black was due to his color-blindness or current events. No matter; the result was striking: darkness in the water, on the fish, covering the shoreline. Enveloped by the dark was a woman with long, curly black hair, wearing a mask and snorkel, diving down to the ocean floor with an outstretched arm. A teacher had written out what Jeremiah wanted to narrate:

"My mother isn't here today because she is closing the hole in the ocean."

The claim was technically false, but the details mattered little to Jeremiah, or for that matter to any of his classmates, their parents, their friends, or the vast majority of Americans. Like them, like all of us, he was just trying to process a confusing series of events that seemed so overwhelming and a disaster management response that seemed so insufficient.

An unnatural disaster not of the government's making, the oil spill nevertheless was a disaster none of us in government could avoid. The media breathlessly wondered, "Is this Obama's Hurricane Katrina?" The fact that the question had to be asked at all was not good. *Close the well*, Jeremiah—along with the rest of the world—seemed to be pleading, a nicer variation of Obama's demand that we "close the damned well." It was clear that we soon would have more than an oil spill on our hands.

David and I hadn't prepared for this interruption, never mind an interruption of this length. Nevertheless, as I always knew him to be, he was sympathetic. We rallied friends and family alike to help with the kids. Later on during the course of the spill, I missed Leo's seventh birthday in May. It was the first time that I had ever been away from my children on one of their birthdays. I told myself he would be fine. I wasn't so sure I would be. I had violated one of my own primary rules: Never miss a child's birthday. There were not many rules left to break.

Day by day, I was drawn into the escalating response. I couldn't extract myself until it ended, however it was going to end. In hindsight, it may seem obvious that we would eventually plug the well, but it wasn't at the time. It was completely possible that the oil would just spill out until the oil patch was depleted, and no one had a clue how much oil the patch contained. Or, even worse, we could too quickly or carelessly try to close the well and cause the ocean floor of the Gulf of Mexico to explode, a catastrophe on a scale never before seen. In those early days, no one knew how to close the well—an effort being led by BP, the only entity with the technical expertise to figure it out. All DHS could do until they, or someone, stopped the gushing flow of oil was to clean up as much of the mess as we could. Which would mean cleaning up a great deal of the spilled oil, but not—it never was going to happen—all of it.

And quickly, I would begin to manage more than seventy federal agencies and offices involved in the spill. I would coordinate with three primary Gulf states (Texas and Florida would see little oil on their shores), their local leaders, and anyone who had a claim on being involved. I would be given a staff and an office at the Coast Guard headquarters in DC as well as in the Gulf. I would never do an interview or go on-air.

I would lead a mini federal department, known clumsily as the Interagency Solutions Group (IASG), to help coordinate the federal agencies that had equities in some part of the oil spill but were not integral to the response. The group reflected the "all hands" nature of the way we would manage the event, and it allowed our federal partners—who didn't know a thing about dispersants—to engage with the response without being a nuisance to responders. Every disaster agency has the mentality of a three-year-old playing soccer:

head toward the ball. The solutions group created a place for everyone to play and contribute but also provided a necessary physical, policy, and geographic gap to give the responders some space. The intergovernmental part of my title was similar to my role as assistant secretary: I would help to manage the politics of the spill through the statehouses and all the local leaders. This was my sweet spot, but the scope and intensity of the spill was beyond compare. Luckily, at first, the oil was still off the coast.

Then on May 19, after weeks of anticipation, the oil finally did hit shore. The first coastline afflicted was Louisiana's, the oil slipping through the fragile marshlands of the Mississippi River. Now we had a spill. Everyone who had been angry became angrier, and the rest of the world caught up.

We tried to ensure that all the agencies were communicating with each other. We began with a call at 7:30 a.m. with the operations team; a pre-governors call at 8:30 a.m.; at 9:15 the governors; at 10:00, a call with the White House; White House meetings or outreach efforts in DC or the Gulf, depending on where I was; a 5:30 p.m. "where are we" call with the senior teams in government; a 7:00 p.m. call with the Coast Guard to regroup for the day ahead; more meetings at 8:00 or 9:00 or 10:00 p.m. Repeat.

Of all of these calls, the governors call was my least favorite. Originally hosted by me, it became so epic that the White House—represented by none other than the president's advisor and friend Valerie Jarrett—eventually took it over to show either their interest or their lack of confidence in DHS. It was never clear, and I never asked. While state operational teams were fully integrated into the federal effort, often the details failed to reach the governors. So day in and day out, Governors Haley Barbour, Bobby Jindal, Rick Perry, Bob Riley, and Florida's Charlie Crist joined a 9:15 a.m. phone call with the senior Obama team to discuss the crisis, the response to it, and their disappointment with that response. Those early-morning phone calls were an important aspect of our communication strategy, but most of the time they left me feeling like I had been tossed into a ring with several welterweights with my arms tied behind my back. Our response was never fast enough, big enough, successful enough. After all, oil was hitting shore.

The governors were not happy. And neither were my kids. One Saturday in early June, I arranged meetings so that I could spend the day with my family. I planned to visit the local pool with my children and dial into the governors' call simultaneously. Not the most brilliant move, but every working mother knows the benefits of the mute button. I was home with my kids, managing towel collection, sunscreen application, and snack packing. And then there was the locating of the Crocs, those oversized and colorful rubbery shoes which make perfect pool footwear.

Meanwhile, I was listening to an update from the National Weather Service to the governors about conditions expected for the next twenty-four hours and how they would affect the spreading oil. Weather and temperature matter in any oil spill: too much wind means that the oil on the water's surface can't be ignited, burned, and evaporated because the fumes may head onshore; too much sunlight means the oil gets loose and slimy and is hard to collect. These were all things I thought I would never need to know.

As the federal weathermen summed up, Jeremiah rushed to the front door, ready to walk to the pool with only one Croc on. He had had them both just fifteen seconds earlier. "Jeremiah," I said, realizing a Croc dilemma could sometimes be as frustrating as anything I encountered at work, "how the hell do you lose your Croc between the kitchen and the front door?"

There was complete silence on the call, which involved not only the governors themselves but also their staffs and numerous federal agencies from the Defense Department to the EPA. Complete silence. I had forgotten to press the mute button. And yes, I did say "hell."

Governor Haley Barbour, a charmer if I ever met one but a political killer as a well-connected Republican, then chimed in. "Seems like we have a bigger mess than this spill, don't we now?" Everyone laughed. I didn't.

The next time I saw Barbour he came toward me with a wicked grin on his face. He leaned in and whispered: "Did Jeremiah ever find that Croc?"

How the hell did he lose his Croc? I don't know. I wasn't paying attention. I was tired and preoccupied. I spent more and more time in Louisiana. The kids ate dinner alone with the nanny. To buy precious windows of alone time, I used TV as a crutch, guiding my children in front of the screen for more hours than I want to admit. They knew, as Jeremiah clearly related in his drawing, that the Gulf oil spill was a mess. I woke up every morning knowing we were in the worst crisis in this president's tenure; every day was a bad day. Our goal was not to make people happy but to make them slightly less unhappy, until the damned oil stopped gushing.

I had no other responsibilities. It was all oil, all the time. Allen was our boss, a tough and demanding leader but also the kind of guy who would randomly pick up the phone to thank a twenty-one-year-old cadet who had just pulled an all-nighter. Peter Neffenger, a rear admiral, was the deputy national incident commander who oversaw operations. I dealt with the civilian and political aspects of the spill. Peter and I testified together, traveled together, and did almost every meeting or phone call together—the political civilian and the Coast Guard admiral. And that divide—between the civilian and the military—proved incredibly frustrating for the civilian in the room, namely me.

For example, there were a number of congressional hearings about the spill. Peter and I were forced to testify in what is known as a "field hearing": Congress held a hearing in New Orleans, all of them coming down to essentially vilify us. At the hearings, however, Peter got to wear his uniform. Lucky him. The members praised the man in starch: "Admiral, thank you for your service." They would then proceed to interrogate me, question after question, dissecting the federal response's failures and transgressions. No amount of calm, reasoned explanation would change their minds. I walked through the list: the ocean was being saved, much of the oil was being captured, and while yes, oil was hitting shore, much, much less of it was appearing because of our efforts. No use.

When the hearing ended, they thanked Peter again for his service. I might have received a nod from one of them; it could also have been a stiff neck. Peter came up to me in the hallway.

"Don't say it, don't say it," I begged.

"You know," he said with practiced exaggeration, "we thank you for your service, too, Juliette."

In no time, tens of thousands of first responders were working the spill response. Our goals were to keep as much oil off the shore as possible by aggressively using dispersants, setting it aflame on the ocean's surface, or collecting it before it landed. Between the governors' calls and the congressional hearings, we were playing high politics as much as we were fighting an oil spill. And in that mess, we admittedly neglected our most important audience—the people who live along the Gulf.

That became clear to me during a meeting with a parish president in Louisiana. That state, like all others, had a complicated local governance system. Other states have mayors or county commissioners, and each of them represents the most granular needs of their communities. Louisiana's system is run, essentially, by parishes.

The parish head turned to me and said the most unexpected thing. "You know," he warned me, "you think this is a national crisis. It isn't. It's ours. And I'm embarrassed."

"Embarrassed?" I replied, shocked at the word. Why embarrassed?

"My wife is the principal of the school. My son manages the grocery store. I work and shop and live here. And I can't provide the basic answers my people want from me. Why wasn't there burning on the ocean last night? Where can we get compensation and disaster relief forms? I can't answer. It's just embarrassing and pointless. If I could answer, I could help relieve your burdens. I want to serve."

I knew the answers to all these questions. We didn't set the oil on fire, a process known as "in-situ burning," because the National Weather Service had declared that the winds were too strong the day before and we worried about toxic smoke coming onshore. Claims forms were available at every library and online. I knew these things. He didn't.

We were missing the most basic point of governance: the people. This wasn't about energy policy or offshore drilling or whether our response was good, bad, or somewhere in between. It was about people watching their lives turn upside down and not knowing what to expect, and wanting to do everything they could to serve but not knowing how to help.

The night after my parish meeting, Allen, Neffenger, and I bunkered down in another hotel room somewhere in Louisiana. It was late. There were rumors that the president was contemplating a different response structure and team—that's shorthand for "we were all about to be replaced." We knew the incredible efforts at play in the response, but it wasn't translating to results that people had confidence in. If they wanted us to pack our bags, I knew I would, at least, look forward to returning to my family. "You don't take jobs like this unless you plan on getting fired," Allen said, trying to make a joke of it.

We were still set to convene the Coast Guard personnel at midnight; somehow we had to overcome the embarrassment—ours and that of the parish president. It goes without saying that we all drank—moderately, of course—that summer. I grabbed a bottle of white wine that was in our room's refrigerator, filling a plastic cup halfway.

"What the hell is that?" Allen said.

"White wine. Chardonnay."

"That's a girl's drink. This is not a girl's-drink night." He threw the plastic glass into the sink and pulled a bottle of Johnnie Walker out of his bag. "This is a Johnnie night."

We then devised a plan over that night that was kind of crazy enough to work. Thank you, Johnnie.

In our earlier efforts, we had relied too much on the governors to work with their locals, the people. We were tied to the states. The laws created after the last oil disaster—in 1989, when the *Exxon Valdez* struck a reef in Alaska and spilled 38 million gallons of oil into the pristine ocean—were solely focused on state-government needs, mainly because there weren't many people up in Alaska and no one had to worry about communicating with locals.

We needed to be more nimble. Instead of fighting the governors, we would speak directly to the parish presidents and their local brethren. We would engage them in the real fight—adapting to disaster—rather than the nightly news fight and the politics of destruction.

And we would do that by putting someone from the Coast Guard in each parish president's office, each mayor's office, each county commissioner's office. A living, breathing, informed person would be on hand to get them the information they needed. If there was oil on their shore, they would know where it was; if there was a claims need among their fishermen, we would get them the money; if there were concerns about closed fisheries, we would find out when they might open. We would go granular. We would go to each and every hometown. We would harness local ingenuity and leadership and give them a way to serve.

One day later, Neffenger and I decided to drive across the Gulf, meeting with every local political leader possible and introducing him to an often unwitting Coast Guard official who would get a desk in his office and shadow him. To say that this was not what the Coast Guard signed up for is an understatement. But we knew that the spill was not just about oil. In a white van filled with Diet Cokes and water, we would arrive at a designated spot to drop off the Coast Guard liaison with his or her designated political BFF; Neffenger noted that he felt like we were dropping off military officials to hostage takers. I thought it felt more like day care drop-off, when your child stares at you out the window wearing a "what the hell" expression as you hurry off, waving. These Coast Guard officials would report to me nightly; at the height of the spill there would be over sixty of them.

We knew that this effort could begin to change the response, and maybe even the narrative. The latter was no easy mission. Anderson Cooper from CNN had found an entertaining and emotional parish president named Billy Nungesser to offer to his viewers. Nungesser, now Louisiana's lieutenant governor, loved the limelight and told stories well. Essentially, the government sucked. He told Anderson that every single night.

I quickly picked Claudia out of a group of men from the Coast Guard. She looked like Kate Jackson from *Charlie's Angels*—my favorite Angel.

"You know Billy Nungesser?" I asked.

"Who doesn't?"

"Can you handle Billy?"

"What do you have in mind?"

"I'm not pimping you out, Claudia. But it strikes me that Billy could use a little attention."

"I know exactly what you mean."

With Claudia's assistance, Nungesser began to understand the complexities of the response and now had a sympathetic listener when he needed help. Within three days of Claudia's arrival, Nungesser was praising the Coast Guard for its responsiveness. Anderson Cooper would not have him on regularly again. Allen, Neffenger, and I were not fired.

And that is how we worked it until the oil stopped coming out of the ocean floor. The panic of those early days subsided; we had a routine and a plan. No effort as big as this one looks good at the beginning, or even the middle or end. But by late May, we had achieved a new normal, even if the oil kept flowing.

Then, out of the blue, on July 15, Allen called me on my cell phone. I was in my car, on Massachusetts Avenue in DC. "Pull over," he said. I found a parking lot in front of a 7-Eleven. It was late. I had just left a meeting at the White House. Tomorrow I would embark on another visit to the Gulf.

"They capped it."

Silence.

"They capped it. They didn't mean to. It's over."

The well had been capped by sheer accident. A measuring cap sent down to determine the pressure buildup took hold and stuck.

Sitting in my car in the 7-Eleven parking lot, I realized that it wasn't really over. Allen knew that. Oil had flowed for eighty-seven days, dumping 4.9 million barrels of oil into the Gulf. Only some portion of the crude had landed on the shoreline, but oil had hit shore. Even with the well capped, more oil would still find land. But at least we knew now that we were dealing with a known quantity of oil. The ocean would live.

"That's it?" I said.

Drumroll, please.

"That's it."

"What do we do now?" I asked.

I had spent days and months in the Gulf, driving from New Orleans to Florida, staying in hotels and holding meetings in local parishes. I had spent nights dreaming of what I had seen that first day, on the flyover, the oil sheen that stretched to the horizon.

I called David. He was awake; he had his own reasons for insomnia. In the midst of my absence that spring and summer, David had had to address a professional issue of his own. His tenure contract with Harvard required that faculty take no more than two years off. He had decided to return to Massachusetts with the kids by September, putting them in sync with the school year and back in touch with their old friends. When he made that decision—not risking his tenure, though he loved his job at the Justice Department—I was still spending most of my time in the Gulf, with no end in sight. Something had to give, and David did. I had learned that something always does.

"You coming home?

"Yes, I am coming home."

"Aren't you supposed to be in Mississippi tomorrow?" he asked.

"I guess I still have to go. But at least there is an end in sight."

"You must be relieved."

"I want to be home."

The oil spill managed to touch on every aspect of what I had come to understand were the basics of disaster management: the necessity to engage local needs and the public's fear; the sibling rivalry among states as they remembered the legacy of Hurricane Katrina; the political gamesmanship played out against the backdrop of a presidential election; the challenges of logistics and moving resources quickly and efficiently; the necessity of triage as priorities were set; the striving for nimbleness as we chased the near impossible mission of capturing oil in water; the lessons learned as we quickly formalized an after-action process to analyze and adapt for the next time; the vagaries of lost Crocs.

We won, in so many respects. It may not have looked that way, but 2010 ended with barely a mention of the spill. It was not Obama's Hurricane Katrina.

There are continuing environmental concerns that will still need to be addressed. But by the following summer, the Gulf experienced a summer surge of vacationers like it hadn't seen in over a decade. Indeed, the economy was so strong that BP requested it no longer have to pay any claims to fishermen, hotel workers, restaurants, and others impacted by the lost summer of 2010. Years later, BP would settle with the impacted states for $18 billion.

I now know that every disaster has two responses. In this case, there was the operational response—killing the flowing well, utilizing dispersants at quantities never seen before, burning oil as it came to the surface, skimming it out at sea, and cleaning it up when it (inevitably) hit shore. And then there was the simultaneous political response that brought into its fold everyone from President Obama and his staff to a handful of cabinet secretaries, the Coast Guard, five Republican governors, and local leaders.

Our operational response in the Gulf was as successful as possible given the magnitude of what we encountered there. But our political response could have been improved. The simple, inescapable fact— that the oil would come, despite all our efforts—was never explained to the public. We never prepared them for what was inevitable: Oil Will Hit Shore. We knew it. The best we could do, and the best we in fact did, was to minimize how much oil would make it to shore. And that was how we would measure victory.

Still, we weren't able to frame the facts—from the disaster to the response and everything in between—in a way that made people understand this was a victory of sorts. Less oil was hitting shore because of our efforts. We had failed to provide the public with the standards of success they needed. All they saw was oil-covered pelicans. All they imagined was the spill seeping down to the bottom of the ocean, as Jeremiah did, dark and scary and lifeless.

Oil. Will. Hit. Shore. If I could go back to that first night in Robert, Louisiana, I would demand that every press release open with this obvious fact. I had to be reminded by a parish president that resiliency isn't just the capacity to respond. Of course, that is essential. But at its core, resiliency depends on a public that is armed with information and a way to engage and, ultimately, is thanked for its service. Localities and individuals—even kids—need to know what is happening simply so they can understand how to help. It is their shore, after all. But if citizens are in the dark, there can be no light at the end of the tunnel. And oil will keep hitting shore, ceaselessly.

GOODBYE TO ALL THAT

with my BlackBerry. When I'd called her office earlier that week, I had told the secretary's scheduler that I just wanted to touch base. I should have lied. When the secretary's schedule was circulated that morning—as it was every morning, to thousands of employees—it simply said, "Meet with Juliette Kayyem: Personal." My staff asked me what was going on, as they had suspicions. David's resignation was no secret. Still, I was nervous. I couldn't find better words to say what I needed to say: I was simply ready to leave.

It wasn't just the oil spill, or the steady beat of disasters that marked so much of my professional life, that had me thinking about my exit strategy. It wasn't just the kids and my desire to regain some semblance of a family life. It was that my continuing education about the nature of homeland security had left me with the sense that I might be able to play as strong a role outside of the mayhem as inside it. And that began at the most obvious place: I needed to be home.

When I told the secretary, she asked if I would consider staying a few months longer, until the end of the year; she was eyeing November 2010 with the keenness of a former governor. Up to twenty-three new governors, many without prior government experience, might be elected, and she wanted me to oversee their transitions into the homeland security apparatus. It was a role perfectly suited to my office and my experience. It was a strong card to play: the homeland transition needed me, and home could wait just a little longer.

We both knew that transitions are always a difficult time, with increased risks—whether the threat was terror, weather, or something else. The governors would pick new emergency management heads, new state police chiefs, and new homeland security advisors. To make the homeland function, we needed to make their transitions as seamless as possible. Each state had different needs and priorities— border states, for just one example, wanted more patrol agents—so there couldn't be a one-size-fits-all approach. My office was to establish briefing materials and reinforce protocols to ensure all would be ready on day one. Adaptability was paramount. And so, as a family, we adapted, again.

I went home that night to tell David that he would be heading back to Massachusetts with the kids alone. Our move wasn't easy for him, either, but he felt that it was important that I stay through this transition. "They always remember your last day," he said. "Exit in the quiet, not in the storm." He knew, as I surely did, that given our experience over the last years, a few months of commuting would be bearable. I gave Napolitano until early December, and then I would be gone.

Packing up David and the kids and the rest of the house in July happened so quickly that I barely remember it. We managed to get a farewell photo with the president. It was a close call, because the boys—high on cookies and candy that I fed them to keep them in line—had to wait for a meeting between Obama and Defense Secretary Robert Gates to end. As their sugar frenzy wore off, they squirmed and fidgeted in the Oval Office waiting area, nearly knocking over an ancient Asian vase. The Secret Service agent eyed them warily.

The photo op took just a few moments. One photograph is a perfect family picture with the commander in chief. But as we chatted, the photographer also managed to capture one where Jeremiah is high-fiving President Obama, Leo has his feet on the Oval Office sofa, and Cecilia—so beautiful, somehow she had grown fast into a young woman in heels—looks shy and awestruck. The president had just asked her about sleepaway camp; he was nervous about sending Sasha. This second image is the only one framed in our home.

And then, just like that, my family left. I transported my stuff to David's parents' house, where I would stay in my sister-in-law's childhood room. My in-laws were generous and compassionate hosts. I thought that I would love my single life: I'd work late, go out to dinner, see movies, drink at bars. But on most evenings, I watched TV with David's parents before heading to my bed. It was hard for me to sleep. The house was too quiet; I missed the sounds of my family close by. Fortunately, on their end, only Jeremiah showed any strain late at night. So we improvised. In their room, where they slept in bunk beds, David taped a picture on the bottom of Leo's bunk so that Jeremiah could look up and see his mother before he went to sleep.

Over the next several months, as I counted the days until I could rejoin my family, David and I learned to adapt to the new situation. We became an even better team. We agreed that the parent-in-residence would take charge; it's just not fair to micromanage from a different area code. David hired our first male nanny—also named David, to keep everyone confused—who kept the boys occupied building tents in the living room instead of doing homework. Again, I learned to let go. The kids were relatively happy to be back home, even if I wasn't there. It was hard to believe, but Jeremiah had spent about half his life in DC. When he returned to our home in Cambridge, he claimed he had no memory of it, a fact vividly confirmed as he searched in vain for a bathroom.

As the weeks wore on and new governors transitioned into office, I began to transition out of mine. Soon, my children knew, Mom and Dad would be normal again (or at least, our kind of normal). We planned, at last, to celebrate Christmas together in December. And there would be no threat of an underwear bomber or a natural or un-natural disaster ruining the day.

Just before I left DC for good, I had one more mission to per-form. I traveled north from Washington to oversee the induction of nearly three hundred new American citizens at, of all places, Faneuil Hall in Boston. Samuel Adams once stood there as he gave a fiery speech to urge colonists to separate from Britain. It is, in some ways, where the colonists became Americans. And now, many years later, inductees from more than fifty countries would do the same, and, as a government official, I would officially welcome them home. DHS has the inconsistent mandate of both enforcing deportations and authorizing induction of new citizens under the same roof. Swearing in new citizens is surely the best power available to a department mostly known for bad news.

As I looked out from the podium, I smiled. I saw an Ethiopian family of thirteen, in colorful traditional robes and head wraps, taking pictures near the podium. Four cool-looking Italian guys in contemporary suits huddled in a corner, laughing. A Mexican woman about to become a US citizen was handing out corsages to her daughters. As I spoke—after a special shout out to the Lebanese in the room—I thought of my own family arriving at Ellis Island (or wherever) many years ago. I spoke to the inductees about how much courage it takes to become a new American, to leave their homelands behind. And I told them that we were grateful for their courage. They do belong. Just as my family does.

The full circle of events struck me mid-speech, and I stopped for a few moments to catch my breath and steady my memory. I thought back to 1995, the year before we got married. David and I had traveled to Los Angeles to visit my family. Aunt Carrie and Uncle Emile lived just a few doors away from Aunt Rosie and Uncle Gene, up the street from Aunt Alice and Uncle Carl, and right next door to Aunt Marion and Uncle Eddie. Eddie, my mother's oldest brother, was the patriarch of her large Lebanese family, the oldest son of the nine children. Eddie had flourished in California, buying a mountain property in a sleepy suburb called Encino well before the valley became popular. Many of his siblings would obtain cheap property from him over the years, which made my visit to introduce David, my East Coast fiancé, just a series of doorbell rings down a slope.

The most important meeting would be with Situ, who waited, standing over my Aunt Carrie's stove, cooking. She was somewhere in her early eighties by then; no one knew her age for sure. She greeted us with heated oil and minced lamb. We were going to make kibbeh, a meat dish with bulgur, pine nuts, and spices rolled into a crescentlike shape, fried, and served in pita bread with yogurt. It is by far my favorite Lebanese dish. David was going to roll and fry kibbeh as a sort of introduction to the family. It was also, surely, a test.

David tried. His rolls were flaky, the butt of a lot of jokes. He played the part perfectly: the outsider nobody knew who was game to cook (a man in the kitchen is often a rarity in Lebanese families), but who could take the ribbing too. Situ laughed, asking how smart he could really be if he couldn't roll lamb.

And then David spilled the kibbeh all over himself. This was actually masterful: Now Situ's cleaning skills would also have the opportunity to shine. David would have to take off his pants—but our car and luggage were at Aunt Rosie's.

It was a warm day, and the steep hill down to Aunt Rosie's was difficult for Situ to maneuver. We walked to Aunt Rosie's together. Situ took out her keys, turned the lock, and opened the door. The alarm sounded immediately, a honking noise that we could barely speak over. We fumbled to find Rosie's phone number, but within a few minutes two private security guards arrived.

David, sporting an oil stain on his khaki pants, began to describe the situation. The guards knew the families on the hill, and while David and I were unfamiliar faces, we dropped enough names from the Encino clan—Eddie, Rosie, Marion, Gene, Carrie, Emile, Alice, Carl, Libby, Edna, Karen, Daniece, Gina, Janice, Eddie Jr., Angelle, Christina, Nicole, Jocelyn, Frank, whomever—that they quickly realized we weren't making it up. "We're here with my Situ," I remarked, pointing to where the five-foot-two-inch Arab matriarch, topping two hundred pounds, had stood.

But she had already bolted to the back of the house and to her room. She came rushing out, waving a Ziploc baggie. "Look, look here," she yelled at them, somewhat angry and accusatory, jingling her gold bangles in the guard's face. In the bag, she had her papers, over sixty years later, including her citizenship forms and passport and some random pieces of old paper that I imagine came from Lebanon. She still carried it around wherever she went. She had two words for the guards, both truthful and shocking: "I belong." *I belong*, she kept saying. *I belong*.

She was home. She had proof.

Years later, standing in front of the new Americans at Faneuil Hall and welcoming them home, it seemed a fitting closure to the loop my family had opened so long ago when they made their journey here from Lebanon. I was now the old guard, and even these new citizens would be replaced by newer ones soon enough. Like Situ, I had clung to my proof. I had taken my own tests and been evaluated. I, too, had had to go through the clearances to enter the homeland. I had the paperwork. And I was ready to pass on the burdens and benefits to others. I was no longer the sole expert.

Not long after that event, I said my farewells to my wonderful colleagues and staff and vowed in my exit interview that I did not possess classified information. I handed in my security credentials. Unlike Situ, I no longer needed proof.

I loaded my car and drove home. I played Rascal Flatts the entire way.

HOME SWEET HOME

IN 1999, I LEFT A JOB IN THE FEDERAL GOVERNMENT TO FOLLOW DAVID TO Cambridge. I was unemployed. In 2011, I was back in Cambridge after working in DC and was unemployed once again. I was repeating myself. But my three kids—healthy, noisy, clumsy, busy, and grateful to be home—kept me occupied. Cecilia, born in an era of little humor, emerged as a funny, sometimes cutting young woman who reads Tina Fey and Amy Poehler's books so she can model her life after their careers; Leo, born during a war and so inevitably an encyclopedia of current events and CNN breaking news alerts, is nevertheless always the life of the party, a history buff and a natural social animal; and Jeremiah, still my baby (though he would protest at being called that), was unfazed by the upheaval of his times and found inner peace by practicing martial arts, telling long stories, and savoring Oreos.

I wasn't plagued by lost ambition. I left government when it felt right to do so, and the decision was based as much on personal exhaustion as it was on professional frustration. I had missed one too many teacher conferences, had one too many post-midnight conversations with my husband. I had lost one—just one—too many Christmases.

I had to try to remember what it felt like to live an ordinary life after so many years focused on extraordinary events. I wanted to read, speak, and write plain English. I wanted no part of sentences that made reference to "cascading losses" and acronyms like "SSI" (sensitive security information), instead learning that "LOL" does not mean, despite my insistence otherwise, "lots of love" but rather "laughing out loud." I wanted to spend my July Fourth celebrations with the kids rather than in a bunker monitoring a huge public fireworks event. I wanted to remember that gatherings of thousands of people are not always occasions for foreboding, but are in fact moments of celebration.

I started running long distance again, retracing my traditional path on the Charles River, past the boathouses and the Massachusetts Institute of Technology and across the Longfellow Bridge toward Boston, looping back on the other side of the river near Boston University and then heading home. I redid our basement, making space for a drum set for the boys. I recommitted to friendships, meeting old friends for coffee and long walks. I dropped the kids off at school on time and then picked them up on time. Cecilia did comment that it would be helpful if I managed to take a shower after my morning run and before my three p.m. arrival, but without a governors call each morning or a classified briefing in the afternoon, the hours seemed to waft by quickly.

We adapted again (again!) to our new normal. I interviewed a young wife named Mallory to help with the kids. She was so kind and qualified, but her best attribute was that she lived on the same street as we did. Reader: I hired her, too (and she is now a part of our family). The first month out I would periodically reboot my Black-Berry, convinced the dearth of e-mails could be explained only by some dysfunction. I spent time in the kitchen and with my family and friends, following the instructions for pesto pasta salads and grilled steak quesadillas. And then one day, just a few weeks into this pace and as if the last two years hadn't occurred, Cecilia asked casually, "So, Mom, when are you going back to work?" And she followed with the even more prescient: "What do you want to do?"

It was a good question. I didn't have an answer.

But Peter Canellos, the editorial page editor of the *Boston Globe*, did. In a February e-mail to me with the subject line "Boston Globe?" he explained that they were looking for a guest columnist. He wanted to know—given my past roles in state and federal government—if I would write one column a week for two months. I could tell stories, Peter said, "stories of what you know." I had written editorials before I went into government service, so, though we had never met, Peter knew I could put something together in 650 words. In March, I agreed to lunch. As we ate Indian food from a lunch buffet for $7.99 at a hole-in-the-wall restaurant near my home, Peter—who had just had tooth surgery, a fact that seemed less strange then than it does now—encouraged me to tell stories of the homeland. "You know a lot," he said, when I wondered whether I actually could say anything new.

And that is what I did.

Eventually, the guest column turned into a twice-a-week column. The New York Times Company then owned the *Boston Globe*, so my pieces were distributed worldwide via their newswire and appeared in the *International Herald Tribune*. It took some time for me to master the structure of a column, and Peter's initial critiques—"You waver too much at the beginning; have a point and stick to it with facts"— still ring in my ears. Other columnists taught me tricks of the trade: if the column can't be nearly written in two hours, then you don't have a point; never write "on the other hand"; don't create straw men; and get off your ass and on the road.

Get on the road? The thought was appalling. I had visited more than forty states and a couple dozen countries in the past several years. I had seen enough. But I soon realized that if I was to tell the stories of the homeland, of the threats and challenges and adaptations occurring both here and abroad, then I needed to go see them. I used the column to tell stories of resiliency, of people and communities practicing grip in the face of tragedy. And I started traveling again, but this time on my terms and with plenty of notice.

Wherever I went, there was still that question, the elusive question every mother, father, sister, brother, friend, and stranger alike wants answered: "Am I safe?" These queries have been about the full array of harms and potential ills that could befall us. Is it safe to travel to London during the Olympics? Is it safe to eat Gulf shrimp after the oil spill? Or—my personal favorite, as it combines parental insecurity with disaster management—is it safe to attend New Orleans's Tulane University so many years after Hurricane Katrina?

Safe from what? I wondered, again and again. Over the ten years since 9/11 had exposed our vulnerabilities, those of us who had served in homeland security still hadn't taught the public about how we judge our successes and our failures. More damningly, we hadn't gotten across the single most useful and empowering lesson we had learned: that the American people—more so than any expert—hold the key to building a nation that can withstand, regroup, adapt, and consequently ensure our own greater safety.

What we needed, really, was just a nation of security moms.

In my columns, I said what I had been unable to say in government: The burden of safety belongs to all of us. We need to know that we will survive and even bounce back as a nation and as individuals. There will be other attacks, or hurricanes, or oil spills, or earthquakes, any number of unpredictable events that will put citizens at risk or, worse—as we learned after Adam Lanza shot twenty children at Connecticut's Sandy Hook Elementary School in 2012—our children in harm's way.

As we have seen over and over again, "Never Again" and "Keep Calm" are futile ways to look at the world, damaging ways to look at a democracy, and passive ways to view a citizen's own responsibility. I tried to show in my columns how we could begin to put homeland security in perspective: Bad things happen, and they will happen again. There will be organized terrorists; summer hurricanes and winter storms; anthrax scares and deadly pandemics; a television network's negligence and a would-be reality star's arrogance; abandoned children in distant lands and massive oil spills in nearby waters. And there is a great, great deal each of us can do to make sure that we regain our momentum as soon and as successfully as possible. We have to see ourselves as a collection of resources that can be harnessed for our own safety and security.

Fortunately, the evidence for this viewpoint wasn't hard to find. I just needed to look and explain. I went to Joplin, Missouri, after a 2011 tornado devastated the town, and returned as it regained its footing and began to rebuild. Joplin had formed a citizens' group based on the input of its residents. New housing ideas and better transportation facilities, a walkable downtown and bike lanes to the suburbs: these ideas were all collected on yellow sticky notes (again, never underestimate the sticky note). Jane Cage, an energetic widow who saw in the tragedy a chance to engage her community, founded the Citizens Advisory Recovery Team, an organization of residents from all walks of life who hoped to use federal disaster funds and business investments to rebuild a different Joplin. The sticky notes formed the backbone of the team's proposals in residential and business development. And then they began to rebuild. Cage remarked, in a line that guides me today: "This is an opportunity that we never asked for, but can't afford to waste."

More stories followed. I watched Hurricane Sandy billow across the East Coast from my bedroom window. I heard in the language of state leaders—led by New Jersey governor Chris Christie, who remarked that holdouts on the shore were both "stupid and selfish"—a call to action. Every individual needed to understand both the gravity of the situation and the limitations of the state's ability to respond. And I applauded the efforts of Occupy Sandy, the spontaneous organization built in the model of the Occupy movement, which used its members' tremendous grassroots skills to help with logistics, planning, and sheltering in communities that were not getting sufficient government resources. Here, citizens took responsibility for their own safety.

I watched the news, in 2012, of an earthquake off the coast of Indonesia, just eight years after a similar quake led to a massive tsunami in the Indian Ocean, killing 226,000 people across thirteen countries. I used it as an opportunity to describe the nature of a "lessons learned" system. Resilient societies are those that remember the past and learn from it.

What can be learned from a tsunami that doesn't happen? For a few hours on that day in 2012, Indonesians feared one would come, but they didn't know, so they prepared for the worst. Since the 2004 disaster, Indonesia had built warning sirens that activated along the Indonesian coast, many of them at local mosques (a brilliant home for an alert system, given the mosques' central role and location in most villages). That day, citizens walked, drove, or biked away from identified risk areas. No tsunami would follow, but no one knew that then.

In some ways, it was a lesson no different than the one learned during the real tsunami in 2004: That year, those who walked immediately away from the water survived. How did they know to do that in 2004? Why did some areas experience massive fatalities, and other neighboring areas did not? Because some Indonesians had learned that lesson from even further back, during the 1907 tsunami. Passed from generation to generation was this simple warning: when the earth moves, so will the oceans, so get to higher ground at once. Newer villages filled with recent immigrants, and certainly tourists, were devastated in 2004 because history had not taught them what was to come. The 2012 response reflected the cumulative learning of a century of disaster; it was only a test, but an important one. Happier outcomes, it turns out, aren't just about luck.

I wrote of the 2013 Super Bowl XLVII "blackout," when darkness descended across half of the stadium in the third quarter of the game between the Baltimore Ravens and the San Francisco 49ers. Yes, it was annoying, but the New Orleans Superdome had seen much worse times during Hurricane Katrina. The thirty-four minute delay in play actually showed how the proverbial "fail-safe" functioned (a fail-safe system is one that, in a failure, will respond in a way that minimizes harm). The stadium's electrical grid was, after Katrina, rebuilt in such a way that any stress on the system would take out only half of it. As I could attest, annoyed sports fans are far, far preferable to citizens panicking in utter darkness.

I used my perch to defend Governor Patrick's decision, in early 2013, to ban all driving during a massive snowstorm that hit New England. It turned out to be one hell of a nor'easter, with Boston's Logan Airport getting nearly twenty-five inches of snow. His decision was highly controversial, but not when put in the context of a city that ought to know better. He was strongly influenced by lessons learned during the blizzard of 1978. That storm was much more than a paralyzing inconvenience; ninety-nine people had died. Fatalities can happen in any disaster, but how and why people die matters greatly for the next time. The 1978 blizzard has been studied for decades to determine whether those ninety-nine deaths could have been prevented. Many of the victims were overcome by carbon monoxide poisoning while waiting for help in their stranded cars. Knowing that one fact, and equipped with the fruits of more advanced weather predictions, Governor Deval Patrick decided to institute the sweeping travel ban. Not a single person died on the roads that day.

I wrote with dismay and anger about the rise of gun violence, school shootings, and our political failures to address the greatest security issue of our time. We may be terrified of terrorism, but any rational accounting of what will likely be the greatest harm to our children always includes guns. My kids learned how to shelter in place in the event of an active shooter, but as they got older and their campuses got bigger, my lessons adapted. If they found themselves in an active-shooter situation, my advice was simply this: If you can, run. And then run faster.

In one column, I challenged the federal government's decision to blindly dole out disaster-relief funds to Colorado and Oklahoma residents who requested compensation in 2012 after massive fires and deadly tornados, respectively, swept through those states. I believe now that to build a more resilient country, we must redesign how we pay for disasters. Our government's disaster-relief program is based on the idea that disasters are flukes of nature, and the law tends to focus on making the victims whole again, exactly like they were before: the house too close to the shoreline, the school with no tornado shelter. We need to reformulate our investment structure to encourage proactivity instead of reactivity and to reward communities that are building better and more resilient infrastructure before disaster even strikes. As a mother, I am a big fan of the idea of the carrot and stick: hold out a trip to Disney World if the kids actually make their beds for two weeks straight without whining. Behavior does not change if we never demand change.

The opportunity I had to write about the homeland let me explain what I knew, and what everyone else should know: Sh-t happens. And from each of those moments in my life, at work or at home, I could remind myself of what I had learned: we must educate ourselves; we must not ignore the signs; we must question our gut instincts; we must get organized; we must prepare to pivot; we must recognize the acceptable losses; we must anticipate the worst; we must prevent the single point of failure; we must redefine success; we must triage; we must communicate with one another. And then we must know, as I certainly did, when to reset.

By 2013, for the first time in years, our family was more than dealing—we were thriving. David returned to the classroom. The kids were happy. I loved the platform my columns offered. As I wrote, I grew more confident and began to explore new issues.

Maybe it was because I had so often been the lone woman in the room that I knew we needed to increase the number of women in all fields of national security. Maybe it was that I increasingly felt that the Pentagon's rule that women could not serve as combat soldiers (though more than 150 of them had died in the recent wars) was archaic, particularly at a time when the lines between combat and noncombat roles in modern war were hard to define. Maybe it was because Cecilia was getting older, and I could no longer keep a straight face when trying to explain why women in the military were not given the same training, the same combat pay, the same combat death benefits to their families, or the same ability to advance professionally even though they were doing the same exact things as men in war. So I penned eight articles forming a damning critique of the Pentagon's old-school policies regarding women in war, often known as the "combat exclusion rule." It was simply time for the Defense Department to change its ways. The combat exclusion rule was a legacy policy that no longer applied to twenty-first century warfare. I was publicly critical of an administration that had offered me so much. I became an advocate for change in a field I knew so well. Reflecting a legal, social, and cultural movement that was demanding reform, I was proud of what I wrote.

In early 2013, the Defense Department rescinded the combat exclusion rules for women. A few weeks later, on April 15, 2013, Peter Canellos called me at 3:00 p.m. to tell me that the Pulitzer Prize committee had just posted their results. I was named the finalist in the category of commentary, based on the combat exclusion pieces. It was an unexpected honor for a new writer. Second place felt pretty good.

At 3:02, Peter called back. "If that was a joke, I'm not laughing," I started. Nothing would prepare me for what he said next, for after years of expecting the extraordinary, I had relaxed into the rhythm of our ordinary life.

"Did you hear about some explosions at the Boston Marathon finish line?"

EPILOGUE

ON THE EVENING OF THURSDAY, APRIL 19, 2013, I EXITED THE TURNPIKE AND waited for the longest red light I had ever encountered. Police cars were now everywhere, and I had already become accustomed to their presence in those few short minutes since the stampede passed me heading toward Watertown. From the corner of my eye, to my right, I could see hundreds of people standing in the large bedroom windows of the Doubletree Hotel, looking down the river at the commotion. Who were these people? Runners who had planned a post-marathon vacation before the bombing interruption? Business travelers waylaid after a meeting? Family members of the hundreds still in hospital rooms throughout the city, discussing an amputation or another surgery needed for their daughter, son, whomever? Mine was the only nonemergency vehicle on the street, a goddamned Ford Escape that couldn't get a quick start if it tried.

The light turned green. I stayed straight on River Street. I hit every red light afterward. I don't know how this is possible, and it has never happened before or since. I could have crossed through the intersections; no one was on the road. But I worried—as I had worried so long ago about putting Cecilia in a car without her car seat on 9/11—that I'd be blindsided and killed for an error that was so avoidable. I didn't like the irony. Not then. Not now.

I hastily parked in our driveway. I bolted to the front door. I imagined someone, anyone could be hiding in the dark. I had just gotten off air, my image beamed to millions across the world, and now I was truly, purely, without question, succumbing to the fear that I had kept at bay for so many hours. It's twenty feet from the end of the driveway to our back gate, and there is no place to hide. No shrubbery. Just gravel. I imagined two men coming toward me from the shadows.

I know my feeling was so irrational. Spare me the risk analysis. For years, I managed my home and homeland as separate and sometimes competing duties. Not this time.

David was waiting up for me. "Are the kids all right?" I asked him. We hugged. We actually hadn't seen each other much that week, as my duties with the *Boston Globe* and CNN had kept me downtown day and night. We had canceled our school vacation trip.

"Bored," he said, "and a little scared, but they are just fine."

Bored never sounded so sweet. I had succeeded at something: I had managed to make my kids utterly bored, so bored they were fighting over screen time and hurling rude insults at one another, and then ignoring one another again. I loved hearing David recount these juicy details. This was perfect—exactly as it should be.

CNN called just a half hour later to urge me again to the studio. They were going back on live with their anchor Jake Tapper at four a.m. One of the terrorists, a man later identified as Tamerlan Tsarnaev, had been killed during a police chase just outside of Boston. His younger brother, who struck him with a car and likely unwittingly dealt the fatal blow, was on the run, having escaped a firefight with police officers.

I finally returned to the studio early that morning and provided a play-by-play account of the unfolding emergency and the subsequent city lockdown. I knew I didn't have to leave the house. But I wanted to. I felt I should because I knew, in some way, I could tell people about their homeland, about my hometown. I had been involved with security planning for the marathon. I knew a lot—I was an expert, after all, and one who intimately understood that marathon route both as a security planner and as a runner. I knew how to explain an incident command system, or the different law enforcement agencies whose jurisdictions span from Watertown to Boston, or what DHS was doing, or what the White House was demanding, or what the CIA was tracking.

I knew the challenges of securing a finish line. Since they are porous by nature and design, the only way to ensure perfect security at one is to not have a marathon. And that is not an option. Because Boston without a marathon wouldn't be Boston at all. We are built to be vulnerable. That's how we run.

By daylight Friday morning, having had no sleep, I was truly taken aback when I heard that my former boss, Governor Patrick, had advised that no one, in a stretch of geography that went from Boston to the outer western suburbs, should go outside. Public transportation would be shut down. Everyone should just stay at home. It was a policy that had no precedent in modern law enforcement. It brought the city to a standstill.

But here's a little secret about that "lockdown": It wasn't an enforceable demand. No law supported it. No legal opinion had been drafted. It was, essentially, a request. And for the most part, maybe the best part, we all listened. We took responsibility for our own security.

Including my kids. Cecilia dutifully warned the boys that even playing in the backyard might be bad. "What if a ball went outside that fence and it bothered the police officers?" she asked them. They played games and watched lots of TV. David challenged himself by finding whatever he could in the kitchen and making a unique dish (kale and tahini?), just as he would during any snowstorm.

I missed all of it, of course. I was just a few miles down the street. I had spent the last twenty months out of government regrouping and becoming the parent I hadn't been able to be while in public service. But when the terror struck our home—our neighborhood—I wasn't there. While this choice was voluntary, I wasn't exactly at peace with it. When a CNN anchor asked me on air what it was like for this to be happening in my literal backyard, I held back tears. I explained that my kids were fine, waiting this out just down the street, but that this was an opportunity for me to explain what I knew to other mothers and parents just wondering what would happen next.

The search ended Friday night, almost twenty hours after I exited the turnpike, escaping those police cars. In a chaotic scene in Watertown, a community abutting Cambridge, Dzhokhar Tsarnaev, the younger brother, was found hiding in a boat that was sitting on the back lawn of a resident who noticed something odd after he went outside for a smoke. Dzhokhar was isolated and shot at and finally captured. Less than two years later, after a criminal trial in a courtroom not far from the marathon finish line, Dzhokhar was sentenced to death for his crimes.

As I was on the air, I would learn that Dzhokhar attended the same school as my kids; he even had the same teachers. The brothers shopped at our market and went to a gym down our street. They were known; they were two of us. They lived and worked just a few blocks away from my house—where my children slept—in our neighborhood, the very neighborhood that came back to its vibrant feel that Saturday morning after Dzhokhar was captured. It felt like a strange awakening after a week of police activity. As my family walked the streets around our home, we saw—more than once—Cambridge's famously liberal residents, many active members of the Occupy movement, offering brownies or a hug to officers walking the streets. Spontaneous applause erupted in Central Square when two fire trucks drove by.

Soon after the week's events were resolved, many critics took to the airwaves to say that the state and city had lost their heads. The lockdown was a concession to the terrorists. The firefight in

Watertown was a grotesque use of force. It was all, they argued, too much.

And maybe they were right. I can't argue against the unknowable: would a lesser use of force have been better? But there was something rather empowering about the city that night. The lockdown didn't seem like just some passive action but rather more a collective decision to stand back as the police focused on an area of a few blocks. Knowing the situation was terrifying for those caught in the secured area, the rest of the city's residents voluntarily disrupted their lives so that others might know peace. I can't guess the result of an alternative scenario. All I know for sure, after all this time, is that Eleanor and La Guardia are never perfectly at peace.

Boston's show of strength in those days—often alluded to with the motto "Boston Strong," or the "Keep Calm and Marathon" slogan that emerged on bumper stickers—actually reflected the investments that had been made in public safety, the professional response, and the demonstrated capacity, for the first time, of citizens to simply stand down when asked. It wasn't luck. It wasn't Zen. This city, my city, deludes itself when we say that we've got some innate Irish breeding that keeps us durable. Remember: not a single person, out of the hundreds who were evacuated to a hospital during the marathon bombing, died. *Not one.* The city's well-honed emergency and health response capacities kicked into high gear. Our resiliency wasn't just a mood.

It was a week like no other, but it, too, ended. And then Monday came, after the Worst Spring Break Ever, and the kids went back to school. We were back to normal, or at least our new normal. The kids complained about the lunches I packed—sandwiches that lacked piz-zazz, string cheese wrapped in plastic, bags of the same chips day after day. Cecilia was late getting ready, again, as she picked out another outfit befitting her unique style. The boys lied to me about brushing their teeth. I cursed that we had no coffee in the kitchen.

As we finally left the house, I could hear the landline ring. We let the answering machine pick up. The school principal was reaching out to the parents through the school's phone tree. In her sweet and comforting voice, she welcomed all of us back to "a great learning environment!" And then: "You may notice a police and FBI presence at the end of the street. There is no immediate danger. The Tsarnaev father worked on this street. As a result, the children will be released on the other side of Elm today. Once again, looking forward to seeing you all for another great week of learning and community!"

David and I saved the message. Something about it seemed to capture the inexplicable moment: our kids, the Tsarnaev brothers who lived down the street, FBI agents on the school's block, and the cheerful voice of a committed educator reminding all of us it was a "learning" day! Her tone made it all seem so natural, when the situation was anything but.

Her message remains on our rarely used answering machine today, more than two years later. I could tell you the litany of threats and fears we've faced since then—the rise of ISIS, the Ebola virus, cyberattacks, the melting Arctic, an unruly Russia, a crazy North Korea, hurricanes, industrial accidents, men who shoot children in their school, Paris, San Bernardino—but this list will never end.

We can't just wait idly for gun reform or the end of violent extremism or the cooling of the earth's atmosphere. We surely know this by now. Yet we can no longer judge our success solely by whether something bad occurs; instead we must also judge it by whether the investments we make in building a more resilient society actually pay dividends. And if they don't, then we regroup, double down, and keep trying to finish the marathon. That is what we owe our homeland and our homes. I simply don't know of a society where there are no monsters under the bed.

"Dang," Leo remarked, as he passed the cordoned-off area near his school. Just a few feet from his fourth-grade classroom, the FBI was quickly assessing and collecting evidence from the auto shop.

"Dang," he repeated. "That's really close. Really close."

It always is.

ACKNOWLEDGMENTS

FOR A BOOK THAT TOOK A LONG TIME TO MATERIALIZE, I FIND MYSELF WRITING
these pages the night before my editor finally puts her foot down. I've
chosen the easier (and fewer-page) route to acknowledge those who
have helped bring these ideas to fruition, from beginning to end. There
are so many to thank for my career—a career defined by so many different jobs in academia, federal government, state government, media, and
the private sector. Many, but certainly not all, are mentioned in the pages
ahead. I am exceptionally grateful.

My agent, Sarah Burnes, likely the most patient woman around, has
been enthusiastic in all my efforts. A mother of three kids herself, she
knew the message I was trying to convey was somewhere in that mess of
material I first sent her way.

To Thomas LeBien, my first editor at Simon & Schuster, who convinced me to come to his publishing house just before he left it. And

ACKNOWLEDGMENTS

then to Marysue Rucci, Simon & Schuster's editor in chief, whose kind but critical e-mail after reading the first draft forced me to embrace the book I was writing. "This is a memoir," she wrote, "so give me some memories." Her team—Emily Graff, Laura Regan, Sarah Reidy, Ebony LaDelle, and Amanda Lang—has been exceptional in these later parts of production from the typesetting to the publicity plan, from social media to the insanely decadent photo shoot that resulted in the cover; they also reminded me that I, use, too, many, commas, as they put this the whole effort into motion. And to my publicist, Michelle Blankenship, whose energy and keen focus have blown me away.

Peter Canellos had more confidence in my writing than I did; he opened up the *Boston Globe*'s pages to help me figure out the themes of homeland security in my columns. He has never given me bad advice, and I never got a chance to clean his office. Susan Glasser deserves a shout out for originally connecting Peter and me. Later, I found several other media homes from which to tell stories of our homeland security. CNN's amazing staff, editors, and on-air talent have been remarkable colleagues, and Nicole Dow has always been close by in that regard. At WGBH, Jim Braude and Margery Eagan give me a chance to riff about being a security mom every week on their incredible show, produced by Chelsea Merz; Phil Redo saw a gem in "security mom" being expanded to a podcast (download it from iTunes!); and my producers there— Abbie Ruzicka, Mary Dooe, and Catherine Whelan—taught me how to speak slower, tell a story on radio, and appreciate hashtags.

After a brief foray into politics that introduced me to committed citizens who wanted to engage, I started my own consulting company to promote resiliency, preparedness, and grip. Dian Lefkowitz—an amazing colleague who never cares when I'm cranky—has steered the team and our clients through many late nights, book edits, airplane delays, and did I mention crankiness? Smart and kind, she is also an amazing mother. Sam Medeiros, our virtual partner in crime, is awake at very odd hours.

On the home front, a bevy of young people have opened their hearts to my family. Cara Fitzpatrick, Annie Robinson, David Alba, and Julie Kellett will always be part of our lives. And then to Mallory Heath: to have you in our lives for this long has been nothing short of a blessing. You have graced us with your "not a problem" attitude. You, Brian, and now Heath are our family.

David's parents, Myra and Jerry Barron, opened their hearts and home to us when we were without a home. We have asked a lot of them, and they asked little in return. The entire Barron clan has given me more love than any in-law deserves: Jen, Jon, Ellen, Jerome, Deb, Gloria, Liana, Rafi, Lily, and Henry.

I love my parents more than I show it, so let me set the record straight right here. There is absolutely nothing they aren't game for; no effort on my or David's part that isn't fully embraced; no event they wouldn't fly six hours to attend; no shade of lipstick I wear on air that my mom doesn't have an opinion on. I think of your selflessness and hope I can mirror it in even single-digit percentiles.

It took me a while to recognize what a wonder my sister, Marisa, is; it isn't easy being the awkward younger sister to her utter beauty, street smarts, and coolness. She has taught me to be a better and stronger person and has never wavered in her support. Her husband, Jamie, and their daughters Charlotte and Lila complete the picture. My brother, Jon, has some fabulous one-liners in this book. He never does anything in moderation. That includes his clan—Paige, Dylan, Britt, Jack, Ellie,

Tegan, and Cooper—who will ensure that the Kayyem name will befuddle TSA agents late into this century.

This book was inspired in many ways by the arsenal of female friends I met in high school, college, law school, work, play, as a mother, and as the wife of David—all of whom I don't see often enough and call too infrequently. You know who you are—the ones who call me when the world seems uneasy. You all are a source of total support. And to the guys, this book is for you, too. Promise.

To my children, Cecilia, Leo, and Jeremiah. I hope you know that these stories of being your mother are only my stories. You have your own. I shared what it is like to be your mother because it is still my greatest success and the part of my life that matters the most. And because I believe that if I can teach you to be resilient and happy (and to make your bed), then you will lead a meaningful life.

And then to David. The love, support, passion, and joy you have given me make it almost impossible to finish this sentence without embarrassing those mentioned in the paragraph immediately above. So I will just say that that was one hell of a tailgate. I have tried to respect your privacy here as much as possible (the few passages with more than a mention, dear reader, required negotiation), but I can't deny that you are in every word of this book. Thank you.

I have spent my career in public safety, counterterrorism, and homeland security, but always in policy jobs. I have not risked my life. I have not saved a child from a burning apartment. I have not been deployed to war. I have watched, applauded, explained, and sometimes even criticized those who serve this nation in every facet of its security. I am grateful for your sacrifices. This is a story about my life in your world, and, through the telling, I hope people can feel it is their world, too.

ABOUT THE AUTHOR

JULIETTE KAYYEM is one of the nation's leading experts on homeland security. She served as assistant secretary of the Department of Homeland Security, where she handled crises from the H1N1 flu pandemic to the BP oil spill. She was also Massachusetts's first homeland security advisor. The founder of Kayyem Solutions, LLC, one of the nation's only female-owned security advising companies, Kayyem is an on-air security analyst for CNN and host of the acclaimed podcast *Security Mom*. In 2013, she was a Pulitzer Prize finalist for her columns in the *Boston Globe*. A graduate of Harvard College and Harvard Law School, she is currently on the faculty at Harvard's John F. Kennedy School of Government. Kayyem lives in Cambridge, Massachusetts, with her husband and three children. For more information, visit www.juliettekayyem.com.